Prayers from the Heart

Also by Lorna Byrne:

Angels in my Hair
Stairways to Heaven
A Message of Hope from the Angels
Love from Heaven
The Year with Angels
Angels at my Fingertips

Lorna Byrne

Prayers from the Heart

Prayers for help and blessings,
prayers of thankfulness and love

CORONET

First published in Great Britain in 2018 by Coronet
An Imprint of Hodder & Stoughton
An Hachette UK company

This paperback edition published in 2019

3

A CIP catalogue record for this title is available from the British Library

B format ISBN 9781473635937
eBook ISBN 9781473635944

Typeset in Sabon MT by Palimpsest Book Production Limited,
Falkirk, Stirlingshire

Printed and bound in Great Britain by Clays Ltd, Elcograf S.p.A

Hodder & Stoughton policy is to use papers that are natural, renewable
and recyclable products and made from wood grown in sustainable forests.
The logging and manufacturing processes are expected to conform to the
environmental regulations of the country of origin.

Hodder & Stoughton Ltd
Carmelite House
50 Victoria Embankment
London EC4Y 0DZ

www.hodder.co.uk

I dedicate this book with peace and love
in my heart to all my readers.

Contents

CHAPTER ONE

Changing Our Relationship with God Through the Power of Prayer

I AM WRITING MY FIRST BOOK OF PRAYERS, AND I AM surrounded by angels, and the Angels of Prayer are here as well. Every now and then, when I glance out the window, I see that never-ending waterfall, surrounding the house and filling the room – going up instead of coming down: a waterfall of Angels of Prayer. I know God has them so close to me, because I am going to write a lot of prayers in this prayer book for all of you.

From the time I wrote my first book, *Angels in*

My Hair, I have received requests from people all over the world to write a prayer book. People have asked me to write a prayer for almost everything you can possibly think of. I know that many of us need a particular prayer for different things in our lives, to help us to cope with life and all its ups and downs.

Even during some of the up times, you can find that you are struggling to get to where you want to be, where you believe you should be. You are halfway up that mountain you are climbing in your life, but when you look forward, you can still see an enormous climb ahead. However, if you glance back for just a moment, you will see how far you have already come, then you can go back to focusing on going forward in your life.

The down times are usually when we are disappointed, because we did not get what we wanted, or we believed that we deserved. You see yourself down at the bottom of that hill, hardly able to make a step forward. Then prayer can help you. It can give you the strength you need, the encouragement to take your next step along the path of your life. This path is always twisting and turning, uphill and downhill at times, while it brings you on the journey of living your life.

We all need prayer. No matter what you say – whether you believe in it or not – there will always be a time in your life when you need prayer. And we do all need it, though sometimes we are so cast down we feel unable to pray. That is why we should all pray for each other, because sometimes we simply cannot pray for ourselves. We may be in too much pain, physically and emotionally, and we cannot say the prayers we need to help us in our lives at that particular time.

Another thing that prayer does for us is to help us all to remember to enjoy every step we take as we walk along the path of life, and not to be in any great rush. Prayer helps to remind us to live life to the fullest, and enjoy every moment; the good and the bad, the not-so-good and the not-so-bad. For all our lives, it is like we are on a weighing scales, as if our happiness is hanging in the balance. But throughout all the ups and downs, we should always try to enjoy every moment, even when we are in tears.

We need prayers for all of these things. Prayers for the hurt and the pain we feel. We need prayers to help us through life, to help us to feel happiness and joy. As we pray, our soul, our energy, becomes connected with God, giving us peace and hope, strength and courage.

All of the prayers in this book have been directed from God, sometimes through the angels. Often, when writing this prayer book, there was an archangel beside me. It was either Archangel Michael or one of the other archangels, and sometimes it was one of the angels that are in my life every day. Of course, my guardian angel was with me the whole time.

Prayer benefits those who suffer with fear, anxiety and depression. A person's state of mind and emotional issues have a physical aspect, too. Both our physical body and our mind need the power of prayer, that connection to our souls that prayer gives. The power of prayer can help us to discover that connection and give us strength to overcome all those mental and emotional issues and, as we will see, this can be part of a physical healing as well.

Individuals need to pray themselves. I know that is a very important part but, as I say, it is important for others to pray for them too, for them to have the strength to deal with what they are going through, and to know they will come out the other side. I have met many people who have said they suffered extremely with mental illness, and some had actually started to think of committing suicide, when one day they found themselves talking to God. They realised that they were praying, and from that day on they had more faith, more belief in themselves. They could see that light of hope in front of them. Prayer helps to lift that cloud, to assist the individual to see their life ahead of them.

How to Pray Better

I just go into prayer. The thought crosses my mind and I start to pray. But many of you ask how to pray or how to pray better.

Say to yourself that you will take even a minute and be silent. You don't have to say a word, only practise emptying your mind.

I don't think you need a specific place. The world has changed so much. People are always moving around. It might be while going for a walk.

There are no bad places to pray. But in some places, the veil between this world and the spiritual worlds is thinner. Some of them, such as churches or holy wells, or sacred groves in woods, caves or mountain tops, have been used as places of prayer for a long time. Such a place has become a holy place, a place of silence, of prayer and meditation, and when we walk into them, we tend to notice that stillness and peace. Most of these are safe places. They have become saturated with the love and spirituality of the people who have been there before. When I approach these places, I see this love and spirituality emanating out from them.

Prayer for Sacred Places

Dear God,
I thank you for all the sacred places around
  the world,
For your angels being in abundance in those
  places,
For blessings that are given of
Peace, hope, tranquillity and healing.
Surrounded by your love,
A place where I can meditate in prayer
And feel the sacredness of this holy place.
Thank you, my God,
Amen.

Sacred and holy places are very important to all faiths and even to those of no religion. They are always full of peace and there are always millions of angels there praying constantly.

Often I will see also the souls of loved ones coming to pray with people. Sometimes, I see saints coming to pray. Even though our loved ones have died, the human body that is the soul lives for ever. Your soul does not die. It is that spark of light of God. It is the spiritual side of yourself.

The soul of your loved one is always there to help give you signs, to whisper in your ear. You can hear the soul of a loved one much easier than you can hear any angel, so listen to what help the soul of your loved one is giving to you. When you feel their presence and you know you should do something, then do it. Say thank you to the soul of your loved one for being there for you.

Emotion makes a prayer stronger. You must mean what you say, not merely repeat things by rote. When you let that emotion pour out, you have started to let your soul come forward. We are used to locking that away, because people from many faiths are told they cannot give out to God, but we are God's children, so we should give out to God like a child, a teenager, even an adult, gives out to their parents. We need to be more open hearted in our prayers. That is what the angels keep telling me. Let the emotions out.

Another important part is that you should be fully aware you are praying, aware that your emotions, your calling out to God is coming from you, from every particle of your soul and every part of your human body. If you are aware in this way, you will find that you are being very truthful.

As you pray more deeply, you will find that you become less aware of your surroundings. You might feel you are saying a very long prayer, but find afterwards that it has lasted only a few seconds.

This is because you were in a more spiritual state. When you notice that, smile, be aware. The world is always in a rush today and we feel we don't have time.

I think every now and then you should listen when you are praying, at the end, or maybe before you say a word.

I believe when everyone listens in prayer and goes to that place of silence, people can hear a voice in a different way. They may be filled with peace and calm, or know what to do or, in extreme circumstances, hear a voice clearly. We do need to take time during prayer to listen. We may hear a loved one, our guardian angel, or our own soul talking to us. We may even hear God talk to us, and if that happens, we don't question it. It is something we just know. It will be clear.

Lots of people ask how often and for how long we should pray. To start out, give yourself a minute to pray and then a minute of silence during your busy day. I know you will soon start to pray more. Even that silence will become prayer, as you learn to go into a meditative state of prayer.

Prayer benefits us all in many ways. Your mental self, your soul, even your physical body. The soul is that spark of light of God. That tiny speck that fills every single part of us. It is part of God Himself, God's heart which is pure love. The more you pray, the more it affects your soul. For a start, prayer helps you to become more aware of your soul and your spiritual self.

You will know then that there is a love that comes from inside you, a radiance of light. As you begin to experience this, your physical body feels different, lighter, physically stronger in every way. It no longer concerns you as much as it would have done before, because of prayer, and that connection to your soul.

You can learn to feel your soul come forward. When someone feels their soul come forward even a little bit, they will enjoy it. They will smile. It might only feel like a second, but it is longer, everything disappears. Your body actually becomes lighter, the aches and pains begin to go away. You may see your soul in front of you, and it is when your soul has come forward in this way that the intertwining process can begin.

An intertwining of the body and soul then starts to set you free. You are aware, of course, that your physical body can get sick at any time. You know you could get all kinds of diseases. You are aware that your physical body will grow old, but because of your prayers every step you take now is different. You feel the power of life itself. You feel the essence of life itself. You discover how truly wonderful it is to be alive, as you are now allowing the eyes of your soul to see through your physical eyes, to see all the beauty in life that is around you.

You can achieve all this through the power of prayer. Your prayer touches your soul, and if your physical body gets sick, but your soul knows you are meant to get well and be here for many more years, you will hear that inner voice coming from your soul, from your spiritual self, saying, 'Let me help you have faith.' Your belief that you have received through the power of prayer will give you the strength to fight diseases that attack your physical body.

Try to pray with a pure heart. When you are praying with a pure heart, mind and soul, it is easy to pray, and the more you pray like this, the more freely the intertwining happens.

I think back to when the Angel Amen was teaching me to pray as a little girl. She said: 'You must pray with no badness in your heart. You have to get rid of the reactions you have to people when they hurt you.' I always say you should take things less personally.

Every time something happens to you that offends you, say that it is all right, I love them. No matter how small or big the thing is, you choose to try not to hate them, to decide to try to love them. I am talking here about trying to love someone while in contemplative prayer, which is about trying to love in that sacred place.

'Lorna, they know no better,' said Angel Amen. I understand those words, but I cannot fully explain them.

A person who prays becomes a brighter person, I don't know how to explain it. It is as if they have started to allow their soul to come forward, so that light is shining brighter from them.

Eventually, the human body will change. When we allow the intertwining of the human body and the soul, we won't get old, we won't become sick. Prayer helps that day to come sooner. It is like a rope, the body and soul becoming one together. How soon that day comes is up to us.

Sometimes when we become ill, or a family member becomes ill, we discover the power of prayer. We pray and ask with a pure heart and mind and soul that God would give us more time. We tell God, 'We want her to get well, if at all possible.' We pray, and our family prays with us. Often this is the time you start to become aware of your soul, but we should not wait until then for our physical body to get sick to become aware of her soul and the power of prayer.

Prayer is a powerful force in the world. I'm always telling people prayer can move mountains, and this is because of our soul – that little speck of God, part of Himself, that powerful force, that we unify together in prayer. We can move mountains. We can make this world like a little glimpse of heaven.

Prayer helps us all and it helps the whole world. We are all connected and we are all connected to all things. When we die, we see this all clearly. But until then, we should pray more and more deeply, so that we begin to appreciate this connection and feel it more strongly.

We don't always know what is best for us, or for the world, but God does. Whenever we pray, we may not be able to move physical mountains, but we are doing ourselves and the world a mountain of good.

Yes, you the people of the world, of all religions and all faiths need to pray more. Prayer is prayer. It doesn't matter what religion you are, or whether you belong to any religion or faith, or not, because none of us ever pray alone. Your guardian angel prays with you, and so do the Angels of Prayer. They enhance your prayer, and so do many other angels that may be around you at that time. They will pray with you when they see you are in prayer. Many unemployed angels, that may only be passing by, will join you in prayer. They become employed for that moment. You may even be walking along the street, and you are worried or concerned about something, and you say a little prayer. Our prayers are always heard. Our prayers give us hope. Prayer helps us to believe that the impossible is possible.

Prayer of Thy Healing Angels that is carried from God by Michael Thy Archangel

Pour out Thy Healing Angels,
Thy Heavenly host upon me,
And upon those that I love.
Let me feel the beam of Thy Healing Angels
  upon me,
The light of your healing hand.
I will let Thy Healing begin,
Whatever way God grants it,
Amen.

I always remember the Archangel Michael standing by my bed, reading out loud from the scroll that carried the words of God for this prayer. Archangel Michael had asked me to do my very best not to allow anyone to change the words because they are God's words. The Archangel Michael was only delivering the prayer, and then I was to give the prayer to the world, allowing you all the opportunity to use this prayer universally, regardless of your religion or what you believe.

This prayer is about the light of God's healing hand, but when you say this prayer, we receive that light of healing that comes straight from God. As God touches us with His hand, He surrounds us, at the same time, with His Healing Angels that comfort us in this prayer.

God is letting us know that He has sent this prayer all the way from heaven with His most powerful angel of all, Archangel Michael. It is a powerful prayer. It reminds us that we must always remember to allow the healing to be whatever way God grants it.

When the manuscript of *Angels in My Hair* went to the publishers, they thought that the 'Prayer of Thy Healing Angels that is carried from God by Michael Thy Archangel' was incorrect English, and they wanted to change it, but the Archangel Michael reminded me, 'Lorna, you must not allow them to change the words, for they are God's words, not man's.'

So I told my publisher, Mark, that they were not to change the words of the prayer. They were to remain exactly as they were. I told Mark why, and he agreed wholeheartedly.

I thank God and all the angels that are here now in the room with me as I write. The scroll that Archangel Michael holds in his hands is so long and it is full of prayers for this book. I thank God for giving me all these beautiful prayers, and the Archangel Michael for telling me to say them in this way. They are written from the heart, in ordinary words that would come from a person's mouth in need of these prayers. They are for you and me. Everyone regardless of what religion you are, maybe even if you don't believe in God or angels, these are prayers for you.

Types of Angels

We pray to God. We don't pray to angels, but we can and should ask for their help, including for help in prayer. These are types of angels whose help we will be calling on in this book. The Healing Angels are tall and elegant. They are radiant. They glow so brightly. They are dressed from head to toe in clothing that looks as fine as silk. Their hands look so slender. Light beams from every part of them.

When I see the Healing Angels, they are usually in groups of about five. They always seem to be very close together and always in prayer. They give a faint outline of a human appearance within themselves. When I see them around someone, giving them healing, they have their hands stretched over the person. It is an incredible sight to see as rays of light come down from the heavens, from God, and go through these angels' bodies, beaming out through the hands of the Healing Angels. It only lasts for a moment and then they are gone.

Each archangel has a commanding presence. They are a powerful force. I will describe one to you – Archangel Michael. When he appears in his full glory, he has a golden crown on his head and a robe of white and gold, which is tied at the waist with a golden belt with a black buckle. His clothes always look as if they are draped loosely over him and come only to his knees. He carries his mighty shield, which reflects radiant light of gold and silver and a sword. Sometimes he will hold them upright and they will glitter like the light of the sun. There are many other archangels whom I have described in my books as well, including the Archangel Gabriel and Archangel Raphael.

There is no other angel in the world like your guardian angel. It is neither male nor female, but sometimes it will give you a feeling that it is male, or sometimes female. Your guardian angel gives a human appearance within itself. It is extremely beautiful and very hard to describe. Your guardian angel can be dressed in a variety of colours. At different times, guardian angels wear magnificent ropes or are dressed in a style that we have never seen in this world.

Your guardian angel is exceptional. Guardian angels are full of so much light, and yet to describe every detail of a guardian angel would take for ever, so I will describe only one aspect of guardian angels – their eyes. They are like the stars in the sky, full of light, but it is the light of love.

On very rare occasions, a guardian angel may give a particular colour to its eyes, but this is very rare. Most of the time, I can only describe them like the stars in the sky. They are so bright and radiant. You can see the love radiating from your guardian angel's eyes onto you.

Your guardian angel can never be anyone else's guardian angel. It only has eyes for you, and you are your guardian angel's number one. It loves you unconditionally. You are unique and beautiful, and to your guardian angel there is no one else in the world like you.

Many of the prayers in this book mention your guardian angel. If you know your guardian angel's name, feel free to replace guardian angel with a specific name. It can make the prayers more personal to you.

We can also pray for the unemployed angels to help us with the trivial things in life. When we feel we need a helping hand in life, they are very willing to help. Unemployed angels are angels that I have seen since I was a child, tumbling down from the heavens. They are magnificent angels. As they fall, it is as if their wings wrap around them, and then slowly they start to open up as they come closer to the ground. As with all angels, their feet never touch the ground. They are radiant with light, giving a beautiful human appearance within themselves.

It is very good to ask the Angels of Nature for help. You can pray to them anywhere, especially if you see nature in trouble or it crosses your mind. They are helping already, but by asking for their help we are empowering them more. We are also giving them permission to push us more, as we are in a sense the guardian angels of nature. We are supposed to be taking care of nature.

There are many Angels of Nature. I always see the Angels of Nature taking care of animals when they are suffering, beckoning to us to help. They are so loving and caring. Sometimes they open their wings and surround an animal as it dies. I know they take the pain away.

The Angel of Water always gives a female appearance. She is beautiful and is like the colours of the rainbow reflected through water. She is elegant and moves so gently, like a wave. She represents all the water of our planet.

The Tree Angel is another beautiful angel. She is only one angel, of nature like so many others, and yet she is in every tree. When I see her, she is so lovely. She is all those amber and green colours of the trees. She moves with the branches. I only see her on rare occasions. (Each animal species has its own guardian angel, but there is only one angel for all the species of trees.)

The more you pray, the more open you become. When you go to a spiritual place, in a forest, by the lake, at the sea, you become more aware of all the angels around you, of the spiritual beings and saints of the past who worked to help nature flourish. You become aware. You start to know. You may look at the tree, you may not see the Tree Angel, but you do see how beautiful it is. You start to pray that it stays magnificent always.

Teacher Angels are always holding something that is a symbol of learning, usually an object that is relevant to whatever they are teaching, or it could be a book or a pencil. Sometimes the angel could be writing on a blackboard. Teacher Angels always have the mannerisms of a teacher, but with great gentleness and love. Teacher Angels are radiant, reflecting light, and sometimes their clothing seems to move a little in the breeze, even if there is no breeze.

Another important angel is the Angel of a Mother's Love. She is round like the sun and enormous in size. Her wings wrap around her, but open out a little, like a mother hen. Her arms are always ready to embrace you in a big hug. Her colour is somewhere between cream and white. She is translucent and you can see a very bright light reflecting from within her, but you cannot see through her.

Her face radiates love as well as light and her eyes are big, like saucers, sparkling with the light of a mother's love. She has wonderful soft curls of creamy, white hair. She radiates hugs all the time. She is so huggable that you want to fall into her arms and hug her and be hugged by her. The Angel of a Mother's Love is there for all of us, no matter how much your own mother loves you, or how much you believe your mother does not love you.

The Angels of Prayer are like a never-ending water-fall that is going up instead of going down, full of the glowing, radiating light of the angels. They are flying straight up to heaven with our prayers, enhancing them.

Angel Amen taught me how to pray as a child. She would sit on my bed. This beautiful angel always gave a female appearance. She looks slender and elegant and extremely pretty. She wears a bright dress that gives a shade of watercolour blue, pink, sometimes even gold. One thing about her dress that never changes is that the top part of her dress is ruched in the old-fashioned way and also her hair flows gently over her shoulders. This lovely angel has always said that amen should be said at the end of every prayer, and if it is not said by us, then an Angel of Prayer will say amen for us.

CHAPTER TWO

Deepening Our Spiritual Connection and Awareness Between Nature, Animals and Ourselves

I HEAR FROM PEOPLE ALL AROUND THE WORLD WHO FIND it hard to understand why some of us are so cruel to animals. When I was a child, if I saw someone being cruel to an animal, the angels would explain that sometimes it is through fear, anger and hate over something that has happened in their life, and that some people feel they have the right to be cruel. They believe that they can take all of this emotion out on an animal, because they experience pain and fear in a lesser way than we do. But this is a mistake.

When you are cruel to an animal, it is horrified. Be kind to animals, even if you are afraid of them. I know some people have phobias. They are afraid of dogs and cats, sometimes birds or spiders, but always remember that does not give you a reason to be cruel. It does not give you an excuse to hurt life. Even if you are afraid of the birds, you can still feed them in the wintertime, down the end of your garden where they won't be near you.

When I was a teenager, a young girl I had got to know had a phobia of dogs. I used to tell her that there was no need to be afraid. If she had to walk past a dog, she was to look straight ahead and the dog would take no notice of her, but on one particular day there was a little puppy on the green playing with some children. The puppy went straight over to my friend, who let out a scream and gave the puppy a kick, hurting it.

The puppy yelped out in pain, and lay on the grass, crying. My friend got a shock and said, 'I really didn't mean to hurt it. I was just afraid of it coming near me and touching me. I'm so sorry.' There were tears in her eyes.

The puppy was surrounded by angels, and I knelt down and touched it with my hands, asking God to take away the pain. A moment later, the little puppy started wagging its tail.

The young children that owned the puppy looked at my friend and said, 'A puppy would never hurt you. He's such a pet.'

The children picked up the puppy and one of the little girls said to my friend, 'Would you like to pet him?'

My friend said, 'No, but I am very sorry. I will never hurt one again.' I saw her guardian angel wrap its arms around her, and give her a big hug.

Angel Jimazen is the massive angel who is the gatekeeper of our planet Earth. He is doing everything to protect it, giving us messages all the time about how important and precious all life is. This massive angel, Angel Jimazen, is dressed in armour of red and gold, with a tint of black, and of course he carries in his right hand that wooden stick, as I called it when I was a child. Some people would call it a staff. It is enormous. Angel Jimazen is a giant. He does everything possible to protect our planet, to quell Mother Earth, but he cannot do it alone.

We ourselves – every single man, woman and child – are the guardian angels of our planet, of all nature. We all need to protect nature, all of the animals of this planet, and that includes the creepy crawlies, those little insects that sometimes we seem to be so afraid of, as well as all the plants, and trees, and rivers. We need nature; it makes our planet a beautiful place to live. We must pray every day for the protection of nature on our planet, and that everyone's eyes will be open, in order for us to take the right steps to succeed in protecting our planet, and all of nature. It means that we will be able to enjoy all of Earth's beauty, and all of the wonderful gifts it gives us.

Prayer for Nature and Our Planet Earth

God, help us all to become the protectors of
  our beautiful planet,
You have given us as a gift.
Open our eyes, and help us to see that
We are the guardian angels of our beautiful
  planet Earth.
There is no need for us to destroy our planet –
Help us to save our beautiful Earth.
Amen.

We have to pray for our leaders to make the right decisions to protect nature and that they will not be overly influenced by the material cost. The people of the world must put pressure on them to make the right decisions. We cannot live without nature.

Prayer for Your Sick Cat

God, I am praying to you every day,
And asking you to surround my cat, who is
    very sick, with your angels.
It hurts me to see my cat in pain
And I only want what is the best for my cat.
I just want to remind you, God,
Please let my cat get well. I love it very much.
Amen.

This is a prayer expressing to God the love that you have for your pet cat, an animal that God has allowed you to become attached to, and it to you. That bond of love that you pour onto your cat, and that your cat reflects back onto you, gives you many happy memories and comforts. The memories may be of your cat lying beside you on your bed, when you were scratching behind its ears, and it was purring while curled up in a ball beside you.

As a child, the angels would say to me that my cat, Tiger, was singing to me. Your cat, no matter what name you have called it, has become a very close friend, and when it is singing to you, it is thanking you for being so kind, so loving and gentle – for taking care of it.

You can be sure when you say this prayer that God

has your cat surrounded by angels to help it and for it to get well, if that is the best for your cat.

There is another prayer I can give you because I hear from so many people who ask me, 'Could you write a prayer for my cat that is missing?' They want the cat they love so much to find its way back home.

Prayer for My Lost Cat

God, my cat has gone missing,
I have looked everywhere for it.
I have called in to all of my neighbours asking
*   have they seen my cat,*
But they all have said no.
So God, I ask you to ask your angels to help
*   my cat find its way back home,*
And if my cat cannot come back home to me,
I ask for it to be kept safe, and to be loved by
*   someone else as I have loved my cat.*
Amen.

To pray for an animal, when it is in need of help, is very important, but even when they are not in need of help, we should still pray for them. They need the protection of the angels, too, but we must remember that we are also the guardian angels of animals. You are the guardian angel of your pet, whether it is a dog, cat, bird, horse or donkey. No matter what kind of animal you have, you are its guardian angel.

One time, our little Holly had surgery. She is our little, white, fluffy dog. She had a lump on her leg, and it needed to be removed. I said this prayer for her.

Prayer for My Dog

I just want to tell you, Lord,
My dog is going for surgery.
I ask the angels to surround my dog,
To hold it in their arms,
And keep it safe as the surgery is being
*   performed by the vet.*
Please, angels, let it be a success
For I love my dog, my Lord.
Amen.

I always remember bringing her down to the vet, because as I handed her over, I saw four beautiful angels put their hands under her. They were carrying Holly, our little dog, just as the nurse was. As I was leaving, I gave Holly a little stroke and told her I would see her soon, and she wagged her tail.

Of course, God knows that your dog is sick already, but as a human being you look on God as your Father. You want to tell God as a child tells a father. You are reminding God even though He does not need reminding, and this helps us to be more involved in the prayer. It helps for our prayer to come from our emotions when we tell God what is happening.

By praying in this way, we are developing a more personal relationship with God. God is not out of reach. It is as if He is standing by the door or sitting beside you. By talking to God in this way, you are adding to the spirituality in the world. That is the way it is supposed to be. We want to change our relationship with God, to become closer. He is your father and also your friend. Today people are searching for that relationship with God.

The angels comfort animals all the time, but when you ask for your pet, especially if it is having surgery, always ask for the angels to surround your pet so that it feels safe. Tell the angels that when the surgery is over, you want the angels to hand your pet over to you, so from that moment on you are your pet's guardian angel and you are taking care of it. You are giving it its medication and loving it. The love you give to your pet will help speed up its recovery.

Sometimes the angels would say to me as a child, if a little animal was sick, 'Just hold it in your hands, Lorna, and love it.'

And that's what I used to do. It worked, and it

always made me very happy. I believe everyone can do this, because we all have that power coming from our soul. The animal may not always get well, but its pain could lessen. Maybe it will die in your arms peacefully, but many times it will get well. There is a spiritual process beyond the emotional happening in cases like these.

When you look at your dog as it lies on its bed after surgery, when it is home with you, know that the angels are still there, helping you to take care of your dog. When your dog is well enough, these angels will leave your dog. I never gave these angels a name, but they are special angels for the animals who are hurt, sick and in pain. They are there to calm them, to take the fear from them. They call us to get help for the animal as well. They are like a light wearing a cloak of gold. They always seem to have long hands, long fingers that reach out and stroke the animal. There is always another dog somewhere else that needs the angel's love.

One thing those angels always love is when the owner tends to their dog and says to the angels, 'You're not needed any more. You can go. I can take care of my dog myself.'

The angels will smile at you, and they will say, 'Thank you.'

They will give your dog the biggest hug ever and your dog will know that when they are needed again, those angels will be there.

These angels are there for all animals: pets, domesticated, and wild animals. They are not with an animal all of the time. They are present only when they are needed, but especially when an animal is dying. These angels are there to comfort them, and help them to pass away peacefully.

Many years ago, I met a lovely young man who had a horse that he loved dearly. One day, the horse broke its leg, and the young man was devastated. He said to me that he prayed and prayed to God – he was begging all of the time, 'Please, let the vet be able to do something for my horse.'

He asked me to pray also. He said, 'Lorna, my horse needs a miracle.'

I told him that I would pray and ask, but as I walked away I said to the angels, 'When a horse breaks its leg, is it not put down? Maybe it's not broken.'

I prayed as I walked along the road. I knew God had the horse surrounded by angels. In the end, God did work a miracle for that horse.

I hear from many people that have horses, asking me to pray that their horse will get well. Sometimes it is that a horse has a digestive problem, and their owners ask for prayers that a solution will be found. Often, they say that the horse is very flighty and they need the horse to calm down, or the horse is fearful about getting into a horse box, because it is a confined place.

Prayer for My Horse

I ask you, God, to surround my horse with
*   angels.*
I'm just asking for one miracle.
Angels that surround my horse,
I ask you to implore God
For that one miracle,
And I ask because I love my horse.
Amen.

Prayer for All Animals

God, please help
All animals suffering.
Send your angels to surround them and
*   comfort them.*
Let their cries be heard by us,
Let man have a heart of love towards all
*   animals to stop cruelty.*
Amen.

Prayer for Angels Comforting an Animal

I thank you, my God, for having your angels
comfort the animals.
I know your angels are there with their arms
wrapped around an animal when it is
suffering.
Your angels are always there by their side when
they are needed.
Thank you, angels, for doing this for all the
animals of the world.
Thank you, my God.
Amen.

From the time I was a child, I have loved that prayer. I have watched the angels comforting animals my whole life, whether it was a suffering dog that may have been knocked down, or an animal on the farm, or a bird, or any of the wildlife in nature.

Sometimes, when I was sitting in the car and Joe was driving, I would look out of the window and I would get a glimpse of an angel comforting an animal, stroking its back. It might be a cow or a horse, and I knew the angel was taking away its anxiety and fear.

The angels are always telling us to take care of nature, to take care of our pets, and if we see an animal that has been cruelly treated to speak up. It is important for us not to be afraid, because animals can be very afraid, even terrified and frightened, when they are being treated cruelly. They do not understand. We know this cruelty is happening all around the world.

I remember Archangel Michael and Archangel Raphael pointing out to me, on different occasions, that if someone is cruel to an animal, then they are cruel to human beings as well. 'Even if you don't like animals and you are afraid, that's okay,' said Angel Raphael. 'Just relax yourself, because the animal is afraid of you, too.'

The angels taught me to be careful of wild animals, and we should all be, but that doesn't mean we should be cruel to the animal that lives in the wild of our country, or take away its home. The angels are always reminding me that we must share this planet with all of the animals of nature.

I often give out to God: if He would only allow everyone to see the angels now, even a glimpse of an angel, and especially an angel comforting an animal when it is in distress. It is a magnificent sight to see, as the angel wraps its arms around the animal and blows gently upon it. This calms the animal. I have seen this happen many times through my life. I have watched it when a vet attended a sick animal as well.

I do tell God that it would be great if we could all see this, because then we would be more loving to ourselves and to nature. We would protect our planet more. There are so many prayers I could write for nature, one for each animal, each bird, or each insect, for all the fish, and all the different life that lives in our rivers and seas.

Prayer for Our Rivers and Seas

Dear God,
Angel of the Water, oceans, rivers,
Wherever water trickles through to our Earth.
Help mankind to listen to the Water Angel
To keep our oceans and rivers full of life,
To keep water pure for mankind and nature.
Amen.

I have seen this angel on many occasions. This prayer is to protect all our oceans and rivers, and everywhere that water trickles through the Earth. I know God has put certain angels around the planet to help nature. I know God has done this to help Angel Jimazen, the gatekeeper of our beautiful Earth.

One of these angels is called the Water Angel. When she comes out of the river and sits upon the rock, she is like water. When she reaches out with her hand to touch mine, water trickles from her fingertips. She is like all the colours of the rainbow: gentle, pastel shades. Everything about the Water Angel is water. She gives her human appearance within it. She is only one angel, but the Water Angel is everywhere there is water.

Sometimes she would tell me how badly the river was polluted and what was happening. One time, the Water Angel came out of the ocean when I was in America. I wasn't expecting to see her, but when I stood on the beach and looked out at the ocean, I was horrified by what I saw. It was covered in oil, and was dark, black and sticky, when this angel appeared for only a moment.

On this day, the Water Angel rose up out of the ocean. I was horrified by how she was dripping oil. Can you imagine it? Can you imagine seeing this beautiful angel rising up out of the ocean covered in pollution? She is part of the ocean and all other bodies of water, because she is everywhere that water exists.

The Water Angel looked like the ocean as it was that day – black, horrible, choking, and struggling to show me what was happening to the life in the ocean and upon it. If she had not been an angel, I would have said she was dying, but angels don't die. Our oceans, the sea, rivers, and streams are all dying because of pollution, and so is all the life within them. Call upon the Angel of Water in this prayer to help mankind to stop polluting our seas.

Long ago, mankind thought we could never pollute the ocean. We believed our oceans and seas were so vast that we could never pollute them, so we kept dumping all our waste into our oceans, thinking we were doing no harm, but now we know. We have polluted and destroyed our oceans, including the fish and the shellfish – everything. We ourselves harvest from the sea, and now we all know we are polluting ourselves and our children, so pray and play your part to protect Mother Nature. Let us all become part of the Angel of Water to protect our oceans and rivers.

Prayer for a Tree Angel

God,
Open my eyes
So I can see the beauty of the Tree Angel in
*   every tree.*
As the trees cleanse the air for me to breathe
Through all the seasons of the year.
Amen.

This is a prayer about the Tree Angel to remind you to protect the trees and how important they are to each and every one of us, and our children. I first talked about the Tree Angel in *Angels in My Hair*. A tree cleanses the air for us to breathe. We make things from it, but our planet needs trees to help the atmosphere to work properly, so that we can breathe clean air and not need masks to keep the pollution out of our lungs.

Without trees, land turns to desert. We would have no rain. We need trees and we need to start planting all around the world, especially the trees that are native to our own countries.

The Tree Angel wants you to see her in every tree, in the green leaves, the red leaves, and so many other colours. When autumn comes, when all the leaves change to brown and gold, and to those glorious shades of amber before the tree goes to sleep – the Tree Angel is still there. Even when their branches are bare and a tree looks quite naked, they are not alone. The Tree Angel is right there asking you to protect trees, because she knows we need them.

The Tree Angel is a beautiful angel, and she moves with the branches and the leaves. She is in every tree, and yet she is only one angel, so please listen to her. Plant trees in your country; trees that are native to your country, because your country needs trees. There are not enough trees on the planet, so please plant as many as you can. Don't allow them to be cut down. Trees should only be cut down if they become diseased, or fall because of nature, or are a danger to life.

Prayer to Implore God

I ask all of the angels
To rush towards heaven
Every single day,
To implore God
For a miracle
For our beautiful planet
And to awaken us.
Amen.

When we pray for Mother Earth, we are asking God to help us to connect ourselves to nature, so that through the power of prayer that is within us, we can protect Mother Earth for the future. When we pray for rain, or plants, or trees to grow, or for our rivers to come back to life, we are part of the prayer which allows that door to be opened. It allows that intertwining of the power of prayer with God, and in doing what we know we need to do to protect nature, we are given the strength to heal nature so that we can live.

Prayer for Harvest Growth

God,
I ask you to give growth to the Earth,
For the seeds I planted to spring through the
   soil,
My crops to grow healthy and strong,
That I will have a good harvest from the land.
Amen.

Prayer for Rain

God, I implore you
Let the rain come.
The land is becoming dry and barren,
If you don't send the rain soon
No harvest will come.
And my family will go hungry,
Nature and all the animals are dying.
Send your angels.
Open the clouds, and let the rain pour down.
I will share my harvest with those in need.
I implore you, God, let the rain come.
Amen.

The more thankful we are, the more we recognise our blessings and through the power of prayer we receive more blessings. It is the only way I can explain the importance of thanksgiving in prayer.

Prayer of Thanksgiving

> God, I am a worker of the land,
> And I thank you for all the angels that you
>   have sent to help me.
> Our animals are strong
> Our crops are healthy, and we had a great
>   harvest.
> Thank you for these blessings and abundance.
> Amen.

Whether you are a farmer, or simply a gardener who looks after the flowers and shrubs, or a person who grows fruit and vegetables for your own consumption and for sharing with your family and neighbours when you have a good harvest – no matter how big or small your role – you should give thanks. I always watch the angels helping people when they are farming or doing the garden.

The other day, I was breaking off the dead heads of the roses that had finished, so that some more could blossom. Every now and then, an angel would point out to me that I had missed one. I know the angels do the same for you. They direct your attention to where it is needed. It might be getting you to look in a particular direction so that you notice something important. They help you to have a good harvest, for a lot of flowers to blossom in your garden.

I know farmers work very hard, and they are always praying for certain weather conditions. Sometimes they pray for rain. Other times, they pray for the rain to stay away, especially when their crops are ripe and they want to get the tractors out into the fields to harvest them. They can't do that when it is lashing rain.

We always need farmers all around the world to have a good harvest of fruit, vegetables and grain. We need their livestock to do well.

I know at times we forget how important it is for the rain to come, and for the rain to stay away, and for the sun to shine. A farmer is always looking for perfect weather so that there is a good harvest. Farmers help to feed the world. They do it through hard work, but also through love for their land and their animals.

When we go to a supermarket and all of the food is laid out in front of us, we don't really think of the hard-working farmer, but I think we should. I think we should say a prayer for the farmers all around the world, so here's a little prayer.

Prayer for the Farmer

God, please protect the farmers.

Angels, rush to the farmers when they are in need of a helping hand,

And if possible, always allow their crops to grow healthy and strong.

Help their land receive the amount of rain and sunshine it needs.

Bless the farmer's land abundantly

To feed my children and the children of the world.

I thank you for the men and women that work the land.

Amen.

CHAPTER THREE

Giving You Strength and Hope

Prayer for Certainty

God,
Help me to hold onto the certainty
That my loved one has a soul,
And is in heaven with you,
And that I will meet them again, someday.
Amen.

WHEN WE LOSE A LOVED ONE AND OUR HEART FEELS TORN apart, it is very hard for us. One thing you need to hold on to, when you are grieving, is the knowledge that your loved one had a soul and lives for ever. They are in heaven, and at peace. One day, you will meet them again. They are not dead. They are alive. It is only the body that has died, but their soul – that little spark of light that God has given to each and every one of us, that part of Himself – means your loved one lives for ever. In this world the spark is tiny, but actually it is enormous. It filled every part of their human body. Their soul possesses every aspect of them. You will see them again, and at times they are right there beside you and in heaven at the same time.

Prayer in Grief

God, please help me
As I sit here at the side of my dying child's bed.
Give me strength. Help me.
Surround me with your angels
As I look at my child, holding their hand,
    kissing them and knowing in my heart,
You are going to take them home to heaven,
And I don't want you to,
But I know you will.
Help me, God.
Amen.

When we know a loved one is dying and that they are not going to be here with us for very much longer, it is a heart-rending thing. For every mother, father and sibling, and for the rest of the family, to watch a child dying is the most distressing experience one could ever go through in life. No one can know, no one can imagine, what this grief is like; only those mothers and fathers who have lost a child themselves. It is horrendous – a mother or father holding their child in their arms for the last time, giving them that last kiss, saying their goodbyes – or a sibling missing their sister or brother for the rest of their life.

The grieving is just as hard for them as it is for all the adults, even the mum and dad. Sometimes adults forget that siblings are grieving too for their brother or sister. They struggle, not wanting to cause any more pain and hurt for their mum and dad, so don't forget to simply ask that boy or girl how they are coping. Do they want to talk? Remind them that their guardian angel is right there with them.

Prayer for More Time

My guardian angel,
Ask God to open my ears a little.
I know you are telling me

> *That my mother's guardian angel*
> *Is holding onto her soul*
> *And it won't be long now*
> *For my mom to go home to heaven.*
> *I am going to miss her so much.*
> *I know my father is waiting for her.*
> *Guardian angel, could you ask God to leave*
>   *my mother here,*
> *Just a little bit longer*
> *Before you take her to that beautiful place of*
>   *heaven?*
> *Amen.*

This is a prayer that you can say for your father or your mother when it is getting near their time to go home to heaven. It might be while you are sitting by their bed in hospital, or at their bed at home, or maybe you are beside them on the couch as they sit in their favourite place. Don't forget to tell your mum and dad that you love them. Don't ever say to yourself that there is plenty of time to do this, you might not have that time, because God could take them home to heaven at any moment. Many of us say we never got a chance to say goodbye.

If no one was there with your mum or dad when they went home to heaven, know that they were not alone.

Their guardian angel was there with them. The guardian angel took hold of their soul, and took them straight to heaven, and they met all their loved ones who have gone before them. Know that they are at peace and that they are happy. They are there with you at the same time, giving you many signs, and helping you through your grief at losing them.

You haven't really lost them. They are alive because of their soul – that speck of light of God that fills every part of the body. Know that they love you no matter what, even if you were not talking to your mum or dad, or if you spoke cross words with them. They have only love for you now. All their questions have been answered. They know God is real. They can see their guardian angel, and your guardian angel too, and your beautiful soul, and the souls of their loved ones already in heaven.

Prayer to Feel Joy

Please God,
Take this cloud of darkness away.
Shine your light upon me,
Send your angels to help me,
Give me courage and strength
To start to feel the joy in my life again.
Amen.

You are asking God to send more angels to be around you, to help you to enjoy life, and to lift the cloud of darkness away. You are asking God's angels to help you to have the strength and courage that you need so that you can smile again, and see that you are loved and cared for, and so that you know your guardian angel is taking every step of your life with you.

Prayer to See the Light of Hope

My guardian angel,
Put your hands upon my eyes,
Just for a minute.
Lift your hands away,
And let me see
The light of hope in my life,
And if it goes out,
Do the same again,
My guardian angel.
Amen.

This is another prayer that you can say to help to lift you out of the darkness, and to see the light of hope in your life. You are asking your guardian angel to intercede for you, to help heal you, and to lift that dark cloud that seems to surround you. Your guardian angel will do this for you constantly, until you come to the moment when your guardian angel does it less and less because you are better; when it does not have to put its hands over your eyes, and then take them away to help you to see the light and all the good that is in your life.

But remember, you have to decide when your guardian angel does not really need to cover your eyes any more, even for one minute, because you have started to recognise that even when your guardian angel has its hands over your eyes and before your guardian angel lifts its hands away, the light has always been burning bright. It has been there all along and has never gone out.

Prayer to Free You from Anxiety

God, please set me free.
Let your angels unwind the chains of anxiety
That are wrapped around me so tightly.
Have your angels loosen them,
And let these chains of anxiety fall away
And disappear.
Amen.

I hear from so many people of all ages and walks of life, doing all kinds of jobs, who talk about the enormous anxiety they have from the moment they open their eyes in the morning and, some would even say, that they have during their sleep. Your guardian angel will always tell you to seek help from a doctor. The angels can help you only so much. You have to help yourself as well, and there is nothing to be ashamed of. There is huge pressure on people in the world today.

Anxiety is a horrible thing to have. Your guardian angel doesn't want anxiety to control your life. Ask God to send His angels to loosen those chains, for them to fall away, so that you can start to live life and enjoy it one step at a time. Remember, you are unique and beautiful, and there is no one else in the world like you.

I know some people that suffer with anxiety cannot even go out of the door it is so bad, but if you suffer in this way take courage, give yourself a chance. Every time you have to do something, and you find it hard to have the courage and strength, say this prayer. Even if you say only one line out of the prayer, God and the angels will know what you mean, and when you stand at your hall door to go out, I know they will help you to loosen those chains of anxiety, to help to give you the strength to let those chains fall away. Your guardian angel will be whispering in your ear all of the time, 'You can do it. You can do it.' Hear the words in your mind, say them to yourself.

Prayer to My Guardian Angel

My guardian angel,
Just before I go to sleep,
Just as my eyes are closing,
And you have your arms around me,
Protecting me,
I want to thank you
For looking after me today,
For being my friend.
Amen.

This is a little prayer, as a thank you to your guardian angel for being a friend, for spending every single day of your life with you, and knowing that your guardian angel will spend eternity with you as well. When you are thanking your guardian angel, you are thanking God as well.

As you walk through this life, know that you are never alone. That God has given you a guardian angel as a gift, and know that your guardian angel can never be anyone else's guardian angel. Your guardian angel is all for you. Your guardian angel only has eyes for you. You don't even have to share your guardian angel with anyone else. You are the most precious thing in this world to your guardian angel.

Remember, you can ask your guardian angel to sit

beside you. Your guardian angel is your best friend and is always there. You can say nice things to your guardian angel and you can say horrible things to your guardian angel. You can give out, as your guardian angel will never take those things personally. Your guardian angel can only love you. It can never be cross with you over anything that you do in your life. Your guardian angel has unconditional love for you. It has no boundaries. No matter what, your guardian angel will always love you and you never disappoint your guardian angel. It looks upon you with a loving heart.

Prayer for Depression

As I struggle out of bed,
I call on you, God,
Please take this depression away.
It makes everything such an effort.
It drains me of energy.
I just want to curl up in a ball.
Let your angels
Lift this depression off of me,
So I can start to live the life God gave me.
I implore you, God and the angels.
Amen.

Depression is invisible to the eye and people find it hard to understand, especially when they don't suffer with depression themselves. Sometimes we think someone is just being lazy, that they don't want to bother doing anything. If you know someone, or think you know someone, who may be depressed, say a prayer for them. Depression can blind a person, and a lot of the time they don't want to live their life. We must all reach out to those who suffer with depression. Stick out your hand, and pray that they will take it. Ask God to lift them out of that depression and surround them with His angels.

Their guardian angel and all of God's other angels are already working very hard to lift that person out of depression. It is only one mental illness, and there are many other illnesses that we can add to the list of mental health problems, but no matter how bad it seems, we can get better, we can climb out of that pit with the help of family and friends and the angels that are in our lives. They are there to help you.

Prayer to Lift the Weight of Depression

Dear God,
Please help me to take one step at a time.
I feel so low, so worthless, and lost in depression.

I know you have my guardian angel carrying me
As I take each step.
Each step feels like a ton in weight.
I know my guardian angel won't let me give
  up
Because you said so, my God.
Others may give up on me, but I know my
  guardian angel won't,
As I take one step at a time.
Amen.

This is another prayer for when you are suffering mentally, or you are feeling so low in yourself, or depressed, or you feel worthless. Remember, you are not worthless. You will get through this part of your life, and you will smile again. You are loved. Your guardian angel loves you. Your guardian angel will help you to take each step, and as time passes your steps will become easier. You will start to feel happier.

Your guardian angel wants you to give yourself a chance, and to reach out for help, so you can start to live life again, the way you were in the past. Know that your guardian angel is helping you each step of the way and is making it easier for you, because your guardian angel wants you to be happy again.

Prayer to Protect My Child

Please God,
Protect my child,
Who is suffering with mental illness.
Let my child come to no harm.
Please let my child know that we love him/
*   her.*
Amen.

This could be your son or daughter who you are praying for. It is terrifying for parents to watch their child suffering with a mental illness. They are so afraid for their loved one. They may even fear that their child might take their own life.

They want their child to know that they love them and that they are there for them. They can ask God to surround them with His angels. They want their child to get better, to be full of life again, back to their true self. I pray this for thousands of people all around the world of all ages, from children to the elderly. That miracle can happen with your help by praying for the stranger, the person you don't know.

Prayer is powerful and many miracles can happen, so please pray for those who suffer with mental illness, and for their families and friends too.

Prayer to Keep Me Safe While Flying

Enormous angel under the plane,
Lift this plane gently like a feather up into the
*   air,*
Angel in front of the plane,
Guide this plane gently like a feather across
*   the sky.*
Angel behind the plane,
Angels under the wings of the plane,
Angels all around the plane,
Guide this plane gently like a feather across
*   the sky*
To land safely,
Gently like a feather,
To land safely at my destination.
Amen.

This is a prayer that I say every single time I fly. I know many people are afraid of flying, or even a little nervous when on a plane. Planes are very safe, but this prayer can help your journey to go as smoothly as possible. It will also help to calm your nerves.

I ask God to surround the plane with His angels, especially the enormous and incredible angel that flies under the plane. This angel is bigger than the plane itself.

There is also that beautiful angel that flies in front

of the plane, parting clouds and easing turbulence. This angel I call on when the plane starts to get rocky, and I ask this angel to keep the plane as calm as possible. This angel gives a female appearance. When I ask her to settle the turbulence, I see her arms come out and go forward, and she parts the turbulence and the clouds, settling the atmosphere around the plane.

There is an angel behind the plane that keeps guard of all the atmosphere around the plane, and those angels under the wings of the plane are there to help the enormous angel that carries the plane, but I have been told this angel doesn't really need any help. It is lovely knowing it is there and all the other angels that surround the plane.

I say this prayer every time I board a plane. As soon as I am sitting on the plane, I will say this prayer a few times. Sometimes, when there is a little turbulence and I see someone getting upset, I say this prayer and I ask the angel in front of the plane, the angel under the plane, the angel behind the plane, the angels under the wings and all around it, to keep the plane flying gently through the air like a feather and get us to our destination safely, and to land again gently and safely.

Of course, when I'm getting off the plane, I always say thank you to the angels, and I thank God for having them there while I was flying on the plane.

CHAPTER FOUR

Prayers of Protection

Prayer for Invisibility

Dear God,
Please make me invisible.
Let me not be seen
As I walk past this danger.
Surround me with the cloak of your angels
That makes me invisible
Till I reach safety.
Amen.

THIS IS A PRAYER THAT YOU CAN SAY FOR PROTECTION IF
you are out on the streets or in the country, and you

need to become invisible as you walk or drive past danger. In today's world, we all need this protection. If you're going down the street, and there is a fight, and there's no other way that you can go, other than past those who are fighting, say this prayer and ask God to surround you with the cloak of His angels to make you invisible from those that are fighting. In today's world, nowhere is safe. At the moment, there is a lot of violence, not only on the streets, but in many other places. Pray as you walk that you are made invisible by God's angels until you reach safety.

This is a prayer that I have told many young people to say, to ask God to make them invisible and to surround them with the cloak of His angels as they walked past danger, so that they are not seen or heard by those who are violent. The angels will blind the aggressors as they pass them by.

Prayer to Heal Those Full of Hate

Dear God,
I implore you to send all your angels.
Help those who want to do harm;
Help them to hear their guardian angel.
Move their hearts with love,

Destroy their anger and hate,
So that they will change their mind.
Help us all to heal them,
So they will do no harm,
And let them know that we love them,
Even though they do horrible things;
Please help us to help them,
My God.
Amen.

Many people ask me why should they pray for those who are planning to do horrible things? I say it is because your prayer could change their mind. Prayer is powerful and it is something we underestimate. The power of your prayer could affect someone who is carrying a bomb or a weapon that would harm men, women and children, and even kill them. Because of your prayer, someone might say something to them that touches their heart, and they could change their mind; healing that anger and hate. We have to send them love.

I believe everyone can send love. You can send loving thoughts. If you can allow your soul to come forward in contemplative prayer, you can send your love. You can picture them; even if you don't know what they look like, you can picture a person with love wrapping around them and touching them with love. You are also asking God to surround them with love so that there is hope they will change their mind, that they will listen, and will feel moved and feel compassion.

Anger, hate and revenge are a repeating cycle. We need to break it with prayer and kindness, by showing compassion and love, reaching out and giving a helping hand; showing that we care and we want to change things for everyone, regardless of who they are. Treating everyone equally with compassion and love is a helping hand to heal all that anger and hate and desire for revenge. It breaks the circle.

Prayer for Those Who Have Committed Evil

Dear God,
Help me to forgive those who have committed
    extreme evil
Even though my heart does not want to.
Please, soften my heart, my God,
Help me to pray for those who are even
    thinking of doing extreme evil.
It's really hard to pray for them, my God,
But if I don't and if I don't forgive them,
I know we have no hope

For they will not listen, then
They will not hear you, my God,
And they will continue to tear humanity apart.
So, I ask you, my God, please help those who
    commit extreme evil to change their mind,
    Somehow, for love to enter them.
Please hear my prayer, my God,
Amen.

This is a prayer we all need to say. We must pray for those who commit evil, for those who create war, for those who kill, for those who rape, for the terrorist, for those who want to listen only to the other side, to evil. We must pray for them that they will stop, they will listen, and will find love and compassion in their hearts. We need to pray that they will not want revenge for things of the past. As Angel Hosus said, 'War is easy to make, but peace is the hardest thing to keep.' It is easy to do evil things.

Prayer for Harmony and Peace

God, send your Archangel Michael
To keep my country safe.
Please don't let there be war.
People of my country need protection.
We don't want war.

In the hearts of the people of my country
They want to live in harmony and peace.
Amen.

This is a prayer I think we ought to keep in our mind all the time. Every so often, we should ask God and all of His angels not to allow war to break out in our own countries. Pray and ask for peace and harmony for all the people of your country, and say to God that you want the leaders of your country, your government or your president, to listen to their guardian angel that there must be no war in your country.

You are praying and asking that when there are problems, they will listen to their guardian angel and the Angel of the Nation, and find solutions. Pray that they will listen to the people of your country as well. That they will care for the needs of their people and for all of the nature and animals of your country. The whole of your country can become one big home for all the people, and be a home that you are proud of, and that you would do everything to protect.

It is so important for war not to come to your country, and that is why the Archangel Michael told me to put the first sentence asking God to send Archangel Michael to keep your country safe.

Archangel Michael is the defender. He does everything to help to keep peace in every country, and yet he is only one angel, helping to unite us all. People believe he is there for them only, but he is here for everyone. Archangel Michael cannot be any one person's guardian angel. He helps everyone equally. No matter what part of the world you live in, please pray that war does not happen in your country. Please pray for all the countries that are already at war, that they will find peace. It is so important.

Prayer to End War

God, please help –
War is tearing my country apart.
The devastation of war in my country is unbelievable.
Children have been killed, and starved to death.
Families have been torn apart.
There is hardly any food or drink.
We are so low, so desperate,
Crying out for help,
But it doesn't seem to be coming.
No one is listening –
God, you are my only hope now.

Please get the leaders of the world to listen,
And stop this war.
Amen.

War causes such horrors, and when you live in a country where there is no war, it is often not something you can comprehend. We are inclined to turn a blind eye. We don't mean to, but we say to ourselves, 'If it doesn't affect me, it's okay.'

We put up a big barrier, an enormous wall between 'them' and 'us'. We do our best not to feel any emotion or hurt about what is happening to people, like us, but who live in a war-torn country, when we hear of their families being torn apart or see it on the news. When this horror is brought to our attention – in a country where there is war – for that moment it opens our hearts and we give a little, but then we close them again.

We go on with our lives and we pretend to ourselves that everyone in the world is living like you and me, in peace and harmony with the normal ups and downs of life. That is not the case in a country where there is such devastation, in a country that is being torn apart by war. There is no safe place for any man, woman or child. Every single day they are living in fear. It is a nightmare that seems to have no end.

This prayer is to remind you that where there is war, the ordinary people need help. They don't want war. They want peace and harmony in their country, but because of politics, power, money and control, many times it is out of the hands of the ordinary people of that country. They just want to raise their family. They want their children to go to school, to play, to laugh, to grow, to have grandchildren, but war does not allow any of this. Never take for granted what you have, because war could come to your country. Let's work together, all the people of the world, for peace.

Prayer to Thank God for Peace

Dear God,
I thank you that the world listened.
There is peace now in my country.
My God, we no longer fear –
Our children have stopped crying.
We have food, water and shelter.
Thank you, God, for sending the Angel of
    Hope to my country.
Now, the world is helping us to pick up the
    pieces.
We start now to live in harmony and love with
    each other.

Thank you, my God, for protecting us.
I work hard now, building a home for my
* children,*
Knowing no bombs will be dropped,
No gunfire will take the lives of my loved
* ones.*
How wonderful life is now.
Thank you, my God.
To live in peace,
Even though I stand in the rubble of my
* war-torn country,*
Means I smile and thank you, God, for helping
* the world to listen.*
Amen.

This is a prayer of happiness and joy, of the end to all the horrors and terrors. Now everyone is living in peace. Even though you stand on the rubble of your city or home, war is over. How refreshing it must feel for all the fear to be gone. No bombs are dropping or bullets flying in all directions.

Now you can start to build a home for the future. The schools, the shops, all of life starts slowly to come back to normal, as all the rubble is moved away, and you start to hear the laughter of children. You know how traumatised they have been, but these children are doing their best to pick up the pieces and make a life. They will help their parents. They will enjoy going back to school, playing games. The men and women will work hard to make their country a beautiful and peaceful place again.

Prayer to Do Good

Help me, God,
To change the world for the better for mankind
*   and nature.*
Send your angels to remind me that I must do
*   good every day.*
No matter how little or small that act may
*   be.*
Amen.

Lots of people say to me that they want to change the world, so this is a little prayer you can say to change the world, to become aware of the environment around you and how precious it is, and how wonderful mankind is as well. With every little act of kindness, we can all change the world.

While one person cannot do this alone, it is equally true to say that we all have an important part to play, and we must play that part every day of our life. We must keep that little bit of consciousness about changing the world, about making it a better place for all of nature and ourselves, in our minds and hearts.

There are many prayers one can say every day about changing the world, but it is important when you say such a prayer that you ask God to help you to change the world with all those little acts of kindness that are so important, no matter what size they are. The world cannot be changed without them. So, when you open your eyes in the morning, ask your guardian angel to remind you that you did say a prayer, maybe months or years ago, and asked God to help you to change the world, to make it a better and more beautiful place.

Ask your guardian angel to help you to start today. It could be by saying a kind word to someone, or giving them a smile, or by helping someone park their car. Maybe you notice someone looking a little stressed over not being able to find a particular address and you offer a helping hand.

Help nature in your garden or in your community. Give nature a little helping hand. Every little thing helps to change the world and make it a better place to live for all of mankind, and all of nature.

CHAPTER FIVE

Prayers for Perseverance, Resilience and Hope

Prayer to Live Healthily

My guardian angel,
I ask you to implore God to send all of His angels
To help me.
I am trying to lose weight, and I am having
great difficulty motivating myself.
Please surround me with as many angels as
possible.
Let my friends hear their guardian angels, so
that they encourage me to lose weight.

I cannot do it on my own.
It's just too hard.
I need help,
My guardian angel.
Amen.

THIS PRAYER TO LOSE WEIGHT HELPS YOU TO SEE THAT YOU need the help of others – your family and friends. Ask the help of your guardian angel to implore God and to have you surrounded by angels. The most important thing about this prayer is that you are asking that all your family and friends, and those that may come into your life, will hear their guardian angels too, and will play their part in giving you the motivation and encouragement to lose the weight.

This prayer helps you to recognise how hard it is and that you may not be able to do it on your own. We all need a helping hand, in every aspect of our lives, and we shouldn't be afraid to ask for it in prayer, and to ask our family and friends to help.

Prayer to Stop Obesity

I am obese, my God,
I hate to admit it, but I have to.
I lost my way and I want to find my way back
    again.

I want to become healthy again.
I am fed up of not being able to do the ordi-
    nary things in life,
Things that most people take for granted.
I have become so fat. I need to say these things
    out loud to you,
My God and my guardian angel,
So I can hear the words myself.
I want to lose this weight and live again.
Help me.
Amen.

This prayer is about admitting out loud, hearing in your own words, that you have become obese. Allow those words to echo in your ears, hear them clearly in your head, and know in your heart that you want to change, that you want to become healthy again. You want to be able to do the ordinary things in life that you are now finding strenuous.

This prayer can help you to think back to when you lost your way, when you started to put on weight. Looking back, you may recognise the disappointment that happened in your life, or that you became depressed or lonely. Admit that it could have been the loss of a loved one or a broken heart.

Thinking out loud, admitting that you want to

change, that you want to become healthy in your body and mind – because the two of them go together – is powerful. I know it is a struggle for many, but I know your guardian angel believes in you, and knows that you can do it, but you must believe in yourself.

Prayer to Exercise

My guardian angel, give me the strength today.
Give me the encouragement to get up and go
for a walk,
To go for a swim or for a cycle.
Send a friend or relative
To call on me,
To encourage me out into the fresh air.
Amen.

This little prayer is about you and your guardian angel giving yourself a little bit of encouragement. Allow the thoughts to go across your mind that encourage you to go for a walk, cycle, or swim, and let yourself hope that maybe a relative or a friend will hear their guardian angel prompting them to invite you to go for a walk with them, to get you out into the fresh air, and to give themselves encouragement as well.

Remember, your guardian angel could also put a

thought across your mind to call your friend or relative and invite them out for a walk, or to go for a run, or a cycle, or an activity of some kind.

Prayer to Help with an Eating Disorder

Dear God,
Hear my prayer.
I have an eating disorder, and it is destroying
   my life.
I have become so unhealthy that I have no
   energy. I just don't want to eat.
I hear my guardian angel telling me every day
   that
I must eat; I know I must.
Help me, God, to eat and become stronger,
   and for my energy to grow.
Put a smile back on my face.
Amen.

This is a cry of help when you have an eating disorder, and you want to become well again. There are so many different types of eating disorders, and I don't know the names of them all. The two most common are probably putting on too much weight and finding it hard not to eat, and the other is not eating and becoming anorexic.

Prayer can help you when you have an eating disorder. It is a cry for help to God and to your guardian angel, but you must remember you have to help yourself as well. You have to want to get well. You have to allow yourself to climb over every obstacle, every day, and do what your doctor and your dietician says, so as each day passes you become stronger and in time, your energy improves. You get that smile back on your face.

We must always remember that prayer can move mountains in every aspect of our lives, but you, yourself, must play your part. God won't force you to eat, neither will your guardian angel, you have to do that part yourself. But knowing your guardian angel is there to help you gives you encouragement and strength.

Prayer to Increase Weight

God,
Help me to put weight back on.
My guardian angel is saying I can do it, so I
*   know I can –*
My guardian angel wouldn't have said those
*   words, God,*
Unless You told my guardian angel to whisper
*   those words into my ear.*

So, thank you, God. I know I can do it. I know
    I can eat and put that weight back on.
Amen.

This little prayer is recognising the words you hear from your guardian angel, whispered in your ear to encourage you to eat, and knowing that you can do it, because you hear your guardian angel's words.

Most importantly, this prayer recognises that your guardian angel would not be whispering these words into your ear unless God had asked your guardian angel to do so. Knowing that God knows you can do it gives you even more strength and encouragement to get back to being a healthy person again, and living your life knowing that you are loved.

Prayer for When Away from Home

Dear God,
I thank you for all the blessings you have given me.
I am away from home and working in a foreign
    land,
And feeling a little fearful.
Please help me to get used to the culture of
    this country.
Remind me to have respect for the people and
    the environment around me.

Help me to feel at home in this foreign land
during my stay.
Thank you, my God.
Amen.

This is a very special prayer for when someone goes to a foreign land, another country that has traditions and cultures that are completely different from their own. It is a prayer of asking God and His angels to help you to understand the cultures and the traditions of the people of that land, and help you to have respect for the people and the environment that surrounds you. Most importantly, it is asking God and the angels to help you feel at home during your stay in that country, so that you can work with the people in harmony and become good friends.

No matter what job you are doing, and sometimes when you work in a foreign land, it helps you to understand how those from another country may feel when they have come to work in your country; that they would feel as you do, strange in a strange land.

Know every time you look at someone in that foreign land that they also have a guardian angel, just like yours; and their guardian angel is whispering into their ear, guiding them through life.

Prayer to Settle In

God,
I am working away from home.
It will only be a short stay.
I ask you to surround me with your angels,
And my guardian angel to keep me safe
Until I return home.
Amen.

Many of us work away from home at different times. Sometimes we do not leave the shores of our own country, but now and then we might have to fly a short distance and stay overnight in another country. This is a lovely prayer that reminds God that you are working away from home, and even though you may only be gone for a few hours, or a day or two, you are asking God to surround you with His angels. You are reminding your guardian angel to keep you safe until you return home.

Prayer for Homesickness

Dear God,
Thank you for my work,
Even though it takes me away from home.
During these times,

I miss my family and I am always homesick.
Don't get me wrong, God,
I love my work and I thank you for it.
When my work is finished
God, just get me home to my family.
Amen.

This is one of the prayers I love myself. It thanks God for the work you have and the job you do but, on the other hand, you are giving out to God as well, because it takes you away from your home, your loved ones, and your country, even though it may be only a couple of times a year.

You are letting God know how homesick you get and how you miss your family, and you are telling God not to misunderstand. You do love your work and you are very grateful for it. You are happy with your work and you are thanking God for all of this.

I just love this prayer. It touches my heart.

CHAPTER SIX

Prayers to Stimulate Family Harmony

Prayer for My Child Working Abroad

God,
I am a father, just like you.
We are all your children,
But I only have one child,
And they had to go to a foreign land
In search of work.
I ask you, my God, and all your angels
Let my child get a job and keep them safe,

And let them be happy and find love.
Thank you.
Amen.

THIS PRAYER IS FOR YOU IF YOU ARE A FATHER CALLING OUT
to God, and even if you are not a father now, one day
this could be you. You are a father in any part of the
world, of any nationality, reminding God that you are
a father, like God, who is feeling brokenhearted
because your son has had to go to a foreign land, to
another country, in search of work.

You are asking God and His angels to help your son
to get work. In that prayer, because of the love you feel
for your son – love that every father has – you are asking
as well for your son to be happy and to find love, because
you don't want your son to be lonely in a foreign land.

Prayer for My Only Son

God,
I am a father and I know you hear from many
   fathers in the world,
And I know every father is your son.
Please protect my son.
He is the only child I have.
Thank you, God.
Amen.

In this little prayer, you are reminding God again that you are a father, but you know God hears from millions of fathers all over the world, every single second, and you know that every father is God's son, but you're asking God to protect one of His children – the little baby boy that God gave you.

You are reminding God that he is the only child you have, and that God did not bless you with any more children, so you are doing your best to protect the one child that God gave you to take care of, and to be the best possible father that you can be.

Prayer to See My Grandchildren

Dear God,
You know I am a mother.
My daughter found love and got married many
*   years ago,*
And a few years later, she moved away with
*   her husband to another country.*
My daughter and son-in-law have two beau-
*   tiful children.*
I miss them, God.
Would it be possible that maybe you, my
*   God,*
Would be able to work a miracle so that

> *I can go and visit my grandchildren and spend*
>   *a little time with them,*
> *Or maybe they will come home to me, even*
>   *for a little while.*
> *Dear God, I know it's a big ask.*
> *But I am imploring my guardian angel and all*
>   *your angels to ask you.*
> *Amen.*

This is a prayer coming from the heart of a mother, telling God how much she loves her daughter, and the man that her daughter married, and the two children they have. As a mother she was so glad to see her daughter in a happy marriage, but she also talked to God about how her daughter and her husband, and her children, had to emigrate to a foreign country, and how much she is missing her grandchildren.

She was asking God if there was any way possible that God could work a miracle so that she could see her grandchildren on occasions and spend a little quality time with them. She knew it was a big ask, but asked God anyway.

There are grandparents now all over the world who do not get the opportunity to see their grandchildren to give them hugs and love. I know we have Skype and a grandmother can see and talk to her grandchildren online, but that is only in countries where that is possible, and it is not the same thing as seeing them in real life.

I say this prayer as well for all grandmothers, so that they can spend some quality time with their grandchildren.

Prayer to Help a Stranger

God, please help me to help a stranger
As often as I can.
Sometimes, when I see a stranger,
I look on them in disgust.
I ask you to forgive me for that, God.
My eyes have been closed and I don't see them
   as a person –
An ordinary person just like me.
God, help me open my eyes and my heart
To reach out and help a stranger.
Just like you would have long ago when you
   were here on earth.
Amen.

This is a prayer to remind you not to have your eyes and your heart closed when you see a stranger in need of help. You are asking God to forgive you for sometimes seeing a stranger and looking on them in disgust or maybe horror. It might be because of who they are or it could be they are a beggar, someone who is so poor or uneducated, or a drug addict or an alcoholic.

You are asking God to change your heart to look on the stranger differently, to see them as a person, and for you to have love and compassion for them. They may only need a little help to change their life and give them hope.

Prayer to Reach Out

Dear God,
As I look at the stranger in need of help,
God, forgive me for being afraid to reach out
    and help the stranger,
But now, as I look at the stranger along the
    side of the road,
I realise that could be my child in another
    country.
My child that has lost their way, cold and
    hungry.
Take away my fear and help me
God with your angels to reach out and help
    the stranger.
Amen.

There is another little reminder in this prayer of how fearful we are of strangers, but yet, when we are standing at the far side of the road and we see a stranger begging, all wrapped in a blanket or lying on cardboard, we must recognise that they could be a loved one.

Remember that this could be your child or your loved one, and in this prayer you can thank God for helping you to understand that the stranger you are looking at on the far side of the road may not be your child or loved one, but they are someone else's. That stranger has a mother and father, a sibling, or a friend, somewhere in the world, and they too are a child of God.

Prayer for Strength

I implore all the angels to ask God to help me
*   to become stronger,*
To do the right thing by others
Even though I find it very difficult
And God, it definitely is not easy.
Give me the strength and courage and confidence
Always to do the right thing,
And not to always think of myself.
Thank you, my God.
Amen.

Many of us have great difficulty in doing the right thing, especially if we are involved in the situation ourselves. We may want to prove ourselves right, even though deep down we know that we are partly to blame. In this prayer, you are asking God to give you the courage and the confidence to make the situation right by doing what is best for the other person and yourself with honesty and truth.

It is about not only seeing the problem from your side, but seeing it from the other person's side as well, and seeing the piece that can be found in the middle that allows you to do the right thing. Whether it is that you know you must take all of the blame or part of it, acknowledging within yourself that you are doing the right thing will lift a weight from your shoulders, making you feel happier from knowing you did it for the best reasons with no anger or jealousy.

You did the right thing because you have love in your heart, and that you always want to have love.

Prayer to My Family's Guardian Angels

My guardian angel, I'm asking you to help me.
I know I ask you every single day,
You know I'm praying to God and asking Him

To *ask the guardian angels of my brothers*
   and sisters,
My mom, and dad, and all my family,
To whisper in their ears
Not to be arguing with each other
All of the time and falling out.
My guardian angel, I would love to see my family
Become one big family, and happy again.
So please, implore their guardian angels to
   keep on whispering in their ears
To love each other.
Amen.

In this prayer, you are asking God, your guardian angel, and the guardian angels of all the members of your family to help to bring peace and love into your family, because you love them and you hate to see them quarrelling with each other, or falling out and not talking to each other for years. It breaks your heart, and you would love to see your family closer in harmony with each other.

Many families across the world ask me to say prayers for them and for the angels to put them on a prayer scroll for them to take to the throne of God. These families often ask for prayers that can stop quarrelling and find peace, and embrace one another in love. I am always telling them to open the door or make a phone call. If the person at the other end hangs up, that's okay. Send them a card and simply tell them you love them.

Regardless of your religion, family is very important. Sometimes we say we get on better with those that are not our family. Sometimes we even say our friends are better than our family, but your family is very important. Your mum and your dad, your sisters and brothers. Remember, you chose your mum and dad. You chose your family before you were even conceived, and you knew everything about them. You had unconditional love for them. As an infant, you have that same love inside of you, so it is still there.

We all need our families at different times in our lives, so open that door. See what you can do to mend the bridge gently. No matter what religion you are, holidays and religious celebrations are a time when you can send a card and let them know you love them, and that they are always in your prayers. Keep the door open. If you have children yourself, let them know about your family, their cousins, their nieces and nephews.

Your children have the right to know all about the family. I have met many cousins and nieces and nephews who said they only discovered each other in their twenties. They never knew about each other, because of family disputes. These nieces and nephews get on brilliantly now and take no notice of the family disputes of the past, so don't deny your children the right to know their family, no matter what has happened.

Prayer for Me and My Loved One

Dear God,
Please help to strengthen my relationship with
  my loved ones.
It is not very strong.
It is always breaking.
I love them.
I worry about them all of the time.
Please surround them with your angels.
Amen.

You are letting God know how hard you find it at times to love those in your life: your family and friends. You have noticed the relationship breaks down and you are asking for strength because you love them.

Prayer for Harmony Between Siblings

Dear God,
I love my sibling, but we are always arguing.
When we talk, we seem to hurt each other.

I don't mean to, my God,
But I always seem to say the wrong thing.
Please help me, my God,
To be more sensitive and more loving towards
  my sibling.
Surround them with your loving angels.
Amen.

Sometimes siblings – brothers or sisters – don't get on together at different times in their lives. This is a little prayer asking God to surround your sibling with His loving angels, and for you to be more sensitive and understanding of your sibling and where you are both coming from, and the differences between you.

Most of all, it is about the love you feel for your sibling and why it is so important for you not to be arguing or hurting yourself or your sibling. It is about sibling love.

Prayer for Sisters

Dear God,
Thank you, God, for my sister.
I just want to embrace her with love,
Because she means the world to me.
I thank you, my God, for my sister,

For she is the best in the world.
I know there is no one else like her.
By the way, her name is _____.
Amen.

This is a prayer thanking God for the sister He has given you, who is in your life. It is letting God know that you love her and want to embrace her in love.

Prayer for Brothers

Dear God,
I want to put my arms around my brother and
   let him know
I love him
He is the best brother in the world,
And, you gave him to me.
I thank you for my brother
And, by the way, his name is _____.
I love him.
Thank you, my God, for my brother.
Amen.

This prayer is for you to thank God for giving you a brother, for having a brother in your life. You want to let God know that you love your brother very much. You are reminding God of your brother's name, even though you know God has not forgotten your brother's name. How could He when you and your brother are God's children. You are telling Him of your brother's loving smile and the jokes that your brother is always bringing up, and when your brother comes to give a helping hand with something that needs doing.

I always feel that it is very important to thank God, and to remind God of our brothers and sisters, of those in our families, and to ask God to surround them with His angels; to keep them safe, and for our brothers and sisters to have as many smiles on their faces as possible, for them to be happy.

You are asking God for them to grow up to be wonderful people and to have families of their own, and for God to bless their families with children, and that they too will love each other the way you are telling God that you love your brother or sister.

Prayer for Your Grandmother

Dear God,
I just want to let you know that I love my
*   grandmother.*
She has been in my life since I was a child,
And now I am grown up and I have a child
*   of my own.*

My grandmother is old and feeble now.
She taught me so much, and I am passing on
    all she taught me to my child.
I love my grandmother, God,
I just want to remind you of that,
And that she is the best grandmother anyone
    could ever have.
Thank you, God.
Amen.

This is a prayer for a mother whose grandmother is very old and feeble. As you reminisce, looking at your grandmother sitting in her armchair with your little girl or boy who is talking to her, you are thinking that one day you too may well be a grandmother. Through this prayer, you are hoping that you will be as good a grandmother as your grandmother is to you. You are simply reminding God how much you love your grandmother and that as far as you are concerned, she is the best grandmother in the world.

CHAPTER SEVEN

God, Help Me in My Grief

PRAYERS FOR THE DEAD ARE POINTLESS, AS THEY DO NOT
need our prayers, but I have a prayer here for those
who are going to die soon.

Prayer for Coming to Terms with the
Fact That You Are Dying

Dear God,
Please help me.
Put me at peace.
I'm finding it really hard to come to terms
    with the fact

That I'm going to die.
God, take away my fear and anxiety,
Of feeling helpless and powerless.
Fill me with your peace and love.
Help me to enjoy the time I have left with my
    family and friends,
To feel your love and presence and your angels
    around me.
Help me, my God, to accept that I'm going
    to die,
To become ready, my God,
Amen.

This prayer is for coming to terms with the fact that you have a terminal illness, or you have been in a horrific accident and you know you are going to die. You feel so unprepared. It can be very frightening. This prayer is to help you not to feel that way, for God's peace to flow over you. Only those who are faced with this understand this prayer.

No one ever dies alone. Your guardian angel takes hold of your soul and those that you loved that died before you are there to take your hand along with the angels and bring you home to heaven in peace and love.

Prayer for My Grandparents

Dear God,

Please send all your Healing Angels to my grandparents.

Lay your healing hand upon them.

Allow your healing grace to make them well again.

I thank you, God, for looking after my grandparents all through their lives.

Thank you, God, for my grandparents.

Amen.

I receive many letters from young people asking me to pray for their grandparents, because they are getting old or they are ill or maybe dying. This is one example of what these young people write:

Please help my grandparents. They have been the best grandparents in the world to us. I, along with my brothers and sisters, love them very much. We spend a lot of time with them. I drop in to see them after school. My grandmother and grandfather always have a snack for me. They haven't been well lately, neither of them, and it worries me.

You see, God, I am only seventeen and I

thought my grandparents would live for ever, but now I'm realising they won't. I just want you, God, to take care of them. My granny's hand was shaking the other day as she handed me a biscuit. I know, one day, you will take them home to heaven.

Please take them very gently when that time comes. I hope it's not for a long time yet, because it's really going to break my heart. I don't know how I will cope losing my grandparents because I love them so much.

This is a prayer from a young person talking to God about their grandparents and realising for the first time that their grandparents were growing old. They never noticed this when they were a child, but now they are a teenager. They are letting God know how important their grandparents have been to them in their lives and how much they and their brothers and sisters love dropping in after school to see their grandparents and sharing all the different family celebrations with them.

They acknowledged all the love and gentleness that their grandparents have shown them. This young person is reminding God of all of this and telling God that when God takes their grandparents home to heaven, it is going to break their heart. This prayer is simply reminding God that they hope it won't be for a long time yet, because they love their grandparents.

When a child is very close to a grandmother or grandfather, and God takes them home to heaven, it is important the adults remember that the child is grieving as well, just like them. Over the years, I have met many children who lost grandparents whom they were very close to and it was devastating for them. Sometimes a child won't talk about it, because the pain was too much. Another time, a child will cry and cry, or the child will become what some parents may call bold, but they are not really.

They are only trying to express the hurt and pain they are feeling, so don't forget to talk to the children about the loss of their grandparents. All through the year, talk about the things Granny and Grandad loved to do. Sometimes, talk about the things that Granny or Grandad did that annoyed everybody.

Remind the children that Granny and Grandad would always want them to remember all the good things and the funny things, and all of the times they spent together.

A Young Child's Little Prayer to God

God,
Why did you take my little brother to heaven?
I miss him.
I look for him every day when I come home
*   from school.*
I keep on forgetting he's gone to heaven.
Could you not have left him here with me?
So we could grow up together?
Maybe when I grow up, I will understand.
I don't now, God, I'm too young.
Amen.

This is another little prayer from a child who has lost a little brother, and is struggling to understand, and asking God why. This child keeps forgetting that their little brother isn't there any more and has gone home to heaven. The child is giving out to God, saying, 'Why couldn't you have left my little brother here with me?'

A child's prayer to God is like a story. These are the words the angels gave me for this prayer. The angel said, 'There are many, many children in the world whose guardian angel woke them from their sleep, telling them to hurry to their sibling's bedroom, because their sibling was going to go to heaven.'

This is a young child's prayer to God about that day.

Dear God,
You woke me from my sleep.
I heard my guardian angel whispering in my
    ear,
'Your little sister is going home to heaven.'
As I opened her bedroom door,
There I saw my sister,
Her guardian angel had its wings wrapped
    around her.
She looked as if she was sleeping.
The room was full of angels.
It was so bright, God.
I ran for my mum and dad,
Trying to hold back the tears.
They came running.
My mum and dad held my sister in their arms.
I stood there beside them. My dad's arm
    around me.
God, my sister's soul was already standing at
    the far side of the bed
With her guardian angel's wings around her.
She looked so beautiful.
As I sobbed, I said, 'Don't go. Please, don't go.'

My little sister answered me back,
And said, 'I have to go. I'm only going home.
I'm not sick anymore.'
She looked up at her guardian angel,
And her guardian angel looked down at my
  little sister.
My sister turned and looked at me with a big
  smile,
And then she was gone.
My God, I just wanted to tell you.
Amen.

The angels told me about these events involving a child telling God the story in prayer about their brother or sister going home to heaven. They are telling God about that night when their guardian angel woke them from their sleep and the young person responded immediately, without hesitation, and was allowed to see the soul of their sister or brother with their guardian angel for a moment. Of course, they asked their brother or sister not to go.

Most of the time when this happens, the young person doesn't remember after grieving, but sometimes it is brought back to their memory by their own guardian angel, or by the soul of the brother or sister whom they have lost, to help them know that they are not alone, that they too have a beautiful guardian angel.

They are being reminded that, one day, they will see their brother or sister again, but not for a long, long time, until they too go home to heaven when they are very old, have loved ones who have passed before them, and might even have children of their own and grandchildren.

CHAPTER EIGHT

Prayers for the Encouragement to Walk Our Path in Life

Prayer for the Unemployed

Dear God,

I implore you to send all of your angels to me.

I am unemployed and I need all the help I can get,

So please, God, send your angels to help me to get work.

I am searching every day, and losing encouragement of ever getting employed again.

I am a good person and a hard-working
person, God,
So please help me find a job.
Amen.

THIS COULD BE ANYONE. YOU COULD HAVE BECOME
unemployed through no fault of your own, and might
have been searching for quite some time for another job,
but haven't been successful. At this time, you are desperate
and you are praying now as a last hope, asking God to
send all His angels to help you to find employment.

Prayer to Find Employment

Dear God,
I am unemployed and I have lost all hope.
I have become depressed and lost.
I seem to be walking around in circles.
I feel I am worthless because I have no work.
Please help me, God, to get a job.
At this stage in my desperation, God,
I don't care what kind of work it is.
I will scrub floors. I just need to be employed
to get back my self-worth.
Please help me, God, to get a job.
Any work will do, God.
Amen.

This is a prayer from a woman or man feeling depressed and lost because they are unemployed and have no work. This is a prayer pleading with God to help them to find some kind of work. In this prayer, their desperation is clear. They do not want to give up the hope of getting employment, saying they will do any kind of work, even scrubbing floors. They are letting God and His angels know that any job will do.

In today's world, the gap between the rich and poor has grown tremendously. We all need to close this gap. If you are poor, it is not your fault that you are poor. It is through no fault of your own, because you work hard. You do everything you possibly can to make life a little easier for your children. You want to see a future, but the world keeps treading on the poor – and we must stop. The world has to change. This is the twenty-first century. Nobody should be so poor that they feel helpless and see no hope. There are so many poor people in the world, and they feel that way. Shame on us all.

For anyone who becomes unemployed, I would ask them not to give up. I know how important it is to be employed. It gives everyone self-esteem. It puts a smile on your face, knowing you can earn your own keep, and that is very important to all of us, regardless of age, so don't give up. Keep looking for employment. If there is any work you can do in your community, do it; so employers can see that you are willing to work.

Prayer for Employers

Dear God,
I implore you to send all your angels to the
*   employers of the world,*
And help them to see that the ordinary people
*   need jobs*
To help the world go around,
And that it is not all about money.
God, have their guardian angels whisper in
*   their ears to give employment*
And to cut back a little on profit.
God, I don't think it's much to ask of
*   employers.*
Work is so important to us all and it would
*   put many smiles on faces.*
I just wanted to ask. Thank you, God.
Amen.

This is a prayer that we can all say to help our world change, to encourage employers to realise that life is not all about enormous profits. We know profits have to be made for a business to expand, but if there is room to employ some other men and women, an employer should do it. In this prayer, you are asking God to help employers to listen to the whispers of their guardian angel and for them to respond. It is a prayer we can all say, whether we are unemployed or not.

In saying this prayer, you are saying it for your future self as well, in case one day you too become unemployed, or someone in your family.

Maybe, if you are an employer, this prayer may touch your heart, and you may find a way to employ one extra member of staff to give them hope and to put a smile on their face.

Prayer to Help Business Grow

Dear God,
I am a business person.
I don't know if you know that, God,
But just in case, I am letting you know anyway.
I am working hard to help my business to keep
  on growing
For those that I have employed.
It is very important to me, God,
That I never have to let go of any of my
  workers,

And that maybe in the future, if my business
  continues to grow,
With your blessings, my God,
I can employ another few men and women,
So please help my business to grow.
Amen.

This is a prayer of a business person. It could be a man or woman. They could be of any age. In the prayer, they are talking to God, telling God who they are and that they work hard, how conscious they are of those they employ in their business, and how important it is to them that the business keeps on growing.

In this prayer, you can see that this business person doesn't want to let down those they employ. They are telling God that they treat their workers with dignity and respect, and that they never want to let anyone go. They want their employees to grow in their jobs, to find satisfaction and self-fulfilment. This prayer shows that letting employees go is a fear of this employer.

This, to me, shows that this employer is a good employer, because they are not only thinking of themselves and of making money or for growing the business, but they are also thinking of their employees and never wanting to have to let them go. They want their business to be successful and are asking God to continue to bless their business to help it to keep on growing. To me, that employer has love for his workers.

Prayer to Thank God for Employment

Dear God,
I am jumping for joy.
Thank you, thank you. I got a job.
Thank you for not letting me give up,
And sending all your angels to help me.
Thank you, God,
That I listened to my guardian angel
No matter how many times I was disap-
  pointed,
Turned down and didn't get the job;
That you, my God,
Had my guardian angel whispering in my ear,
'Keep looking, keep looking,'
And now, I jump for joy, God.
I thank you so much.
At long last, I have a job.
Thank you, my God.
Amen.

This is a prayer about someone finding employment and thanking God that no matter how many times they were turned down, they didn't give up. God had their guardian angel constantly whispering in their ear, 'Keep looking, keep looking.'

Sometimes the message God has your guardian angel whisper in your year can be so simple, like 'Keep looking.' It could have been, 'Don't give up.' These words could have been whispered by your guardian angel to encourage you, and now you are jumping for joy because you have employment. You are letting God know how much you appreciate getting a job, and how wonderful it is, and what it means to you. At the same time, you are saying thank you to your guardian angel and all the other angels. As well as that, you are saying thank you to your employer.

Prayer for Help in My New Job

Dear God,
Thank you for my new job;
Thank you for my new employer;
For giving me a chance to work.
Help me to show my new employer
That I am worth it, God.

> *Keep on having my guardian angel whisper in*
>   *my ear*
> *That I must do my job to the best of my ability.*
> *Thank you, God.*
> *Amen.*

This is only a short little prayer. You have found employment, and are again thanking God for your new job. That is, you are thanking God as well for the person who has just employed you, and you are asking God to keep your guardian angel whispering in your ear to support you in doing your new job to the best of your ability, always.

It is a simple prayer, and I guess, many times, when we are employed, we forget about our new employer. We forget to thank God for them, for giving you the opportunity, for a new employer choosing you out of so many other people that may have gone for the same job.

Prayer to Help Others Find Work

> *God,*
> *I have my new job now,*
> *But I was thinking, God,*
> *About all of the other men and women*
> *That went for the same job as I*
> *And were turned down.*

My heart feels sad for them,
And I ask you, God,
If at all possible,
Could you help all of those men and women
to get a job as well.
God,
I would really appreciate that.
Amen.

This is a person in prayer who is overjoyed about their new job, and yet their heart is moved, knowing that many others went for the same job as themselves and didn't get it. I think that this is a lovely prayer; someone is asking God that all of those other men and women find a job too, even though they didn't get the job that he or she has. They are expressing to God how much they would appreciate it if all those men and women could find a job as soon as possible.

To me, this is a lovely prayer of one not thinking of themselves, but of all the other men and women and how much they were in hope, praying and asking God and the angels to help them to get the same job; but there was only one job and only one person could get it. They are acknowledging how grateful they are for the job, while still remembering all the other men and women, even though they are strangers to them, who missed out.

Prayer for the Homeless

Dear guardian angel,
I need your help.
I'm lost and homeless and I don't know what
  to do.
I thank God for all he has given me in my life.
I just need a helping hand to get off the streets
  and to have a roof over my head.
I will work with God's plan, whatever it is.
Let God know, my guardian angel, that I'm
  ready to listen.
Amen.

This is a prayer from someone who is homeless. You can imagine them sleeping on the street, with a blanket wrapped around them and with newspapers under them. They are praying to God asking for help to get out of the cold and the rain. They want a roof over their head and their life back. They are asking their guardian angel to tell God that they are ready to listen to whatever plans God has for them, and that they will play their part in the hopes of having a roof over their head, to not be homeless any more.

No one should be homeless. We should all have a home. It is a human right, and we all know this.

Prayer for Financial Help

Dear God,
I thank you for all the material things that
*   you have given me already in this life.*
I need your help, my God,
Help me to listen to my guardian angel,
Help me to look for help and guidance to get
*   out of this mess.*
Shine the light upon the road for me to follow,
*   my God,*
To find the financial help I need.
Thank you, my God.
Amen.

Most of us worry about financial things, about money, and this is a little prayer which asks God for help to see the light that will help you go in the right direction to sort out your financial difficulties. It is about realising that you cannot do it on your own and that you must have the courage to ask for help from the angels, from God, and especially from people. You are already asking for God's help, and your guardian angel is encouraging you.

Sometimes money worries may seem small to others, but they are very big to ourselves. You could be a mother or father, who sees no way to find the money for a pair of school shoes, or are having difficulty paying your electricity bill. Don't be afraid to ask for help.

God will always help you to find a way to sort it out and your guardian angel will do everything to help you to listen for where to go and what to do.

Prayer to Sell My House

Dear God,
I implore you, God, to have your angels
surround my house now.
Allow the love that has been in the house for
generations
Touch those who come to view it;
That they may buy the house that you blessed
with love.
Have your angels, God, in every corner of
every room.
Let my house sell.
I thank you, God, for everything.
Amen.

When you have to sell a house and move home, it can be very stressful. Many of us have to move home for different reasons and the sale of one's home is very important. This is a prayer to ask God to let your house sell; for God to allow His love and light shine from it, so that when people go in to view the house, they feel that warmth of love. Hopefully, they will feel that the house is full of warmth and they can see themselves making it into their new home.

Prayer for the Sale of a Home

Dear God,
Thank you, God, in advance for the sale of
my home.
I feel a little sad now, God, having to leave it
Because of all the many happy memories.
Bless it for the new family and fill it with your
angels, my God.
Fill it with love, happiness and joy.
Thank you, my God.
Amen.

This is a prayer thanking God in advance of the sale of your home. It allows God to know that you believe your home will sell, that you trust and that you have done everything that needs to be done for the sale of your home, and you are just thanking Him in advance.

Trust and belief helps to empower your prayer. You are doing everything in your power to promote and sell your house. You need to play your part as well.

The more you get used to praying, the more you grow spiritually. You are talking with God every day. You are becoming more spiritual, more trusting, and your belief will grow. You could be on a train, a bus, or in a pub. You are communicating with God. You can ask for belief in God through your prayers.

While saying this prayer, allow all the happy memories of being in that home to cross your mind and think of whoever the new owners may be. You know you will be leaving soon, and you are asking God to bless the house for the new family who will move in. You are asking God to fill it with His angels, and for them to bring love and happiness and joy into the home. You are wishing whoever buys your house all the blessings possible.

CHAPTER NINE

Peer Pressure, Addiction and Supporting your Loved Ones

Prayer to Help with Drug Addiction
or Alcoholism

Dear God,
I am a drug addict/alcoholic
And I don't know how to help myself.
I know you have me surrounded by your
angels.
I know my guardian angel is always whispering
in my ear

That I can get off the drugs/alcohol, that I
 can do it,
But I am not listening,
And I ask you, my God,
Please help me to listen
To hear the words of my guardian angel
And to believe I can do it.
Amen.

THIS IS A PRAYER OF A DRUG ADDICT OR ALCOHOLIC acknowledging for the first time that they have a problem. Through this prayer, they are telling God that they really don't know how to help themselves, even though they are aware of their guardian angel, who is reminding them every day that they can get off the drugs or alcohol. This person does not feel that they have the courage and strength to do so, so they are asking God to help them to really listen, to really hear their guardian angel, and believe in themselves that they can do it. The first step is always the hardest for a drug addict or an alcoholic.

The angels are always telling me that drug addicts can get off drugs, but they must take one day at a time. If you are addicted to drugs, I believe you can do it, so please, believe in yourself.

Prayer to Free Me from Drug Addiction or Alcoholism

Dear God,

I have been so foolish.

I wasn't listening to you, God, or to my guardian angel

When some of my friends were pressuring me,

'Come on, just try it. It's good. It'll do you no harm.'

I just wanted to fit in, God,

And I heard you all the time saying no,

But I went ahead and did it.

I took the drug or drank the alcohol,

And now the drug/alcohol has me in a prison.

Help me, God, and all your angels

To get me out of this prison, to free myself of this drug addiction/alcoholism.

I want my life back.

Please God, help me.

Amen.

So many young people can be led into drugs or alcoholism, especially when they start out on life. They want to have a good time and have fun, and it is so easy to get involved in drugs or drink excessive amounts of alcohol these days, because they are everywhere. It is not only among the young people, but also those who are older. There is a lot of talk saying that these drugs or alcohol will do you no harm and you will be okay, you won't even need to try it a second time, but that is not the way it always works out.

Even though this young person heard God and her guardian angel saying, 'No, don't try the drug,' which her friend was offering, she did. It was because she wanted to fit in with her new friends. The one thing young people want is to be accepted, but I tell them, 'Just be yourself. Don't try to be anyone else, and you will fit in.'

It is hard for a young person to say no. When they do, I think it shows great strength of character. That young person stands out. I believe that those who don't follow the crowd are the ones who make the difference in the world, because they are not afraid to say no when they know something is wrong, unjust, or immoral.

All of us need to pray for the young people in the world today, and even those that are older, who get tangled up in the bad influences of the world.

Life should be lived to the fullest. Pray to God to give them strength to say no and to be themselves – to be the wonderful human being that they are.

Prayer to Help Those with Addiction

Dear God,
I implore you,
Please send all your angels to help me
So that I can prove to those that love me
That I want to give up the drugs/alcohol.
With your angels' help, free me from the drugs/
  alcohol.
I am desperate, God.
Look at me –
I am shaking.
I am in tears.
If I continue living like this,
I will lose my family, my children, my friends,
  all those that love me.
God, don't let those that love me give up on me.
Please help me. Don't abandon me, my God.
Amen.

When someone is sitting alone, shaking and trembling in tears, this prayer is for them. They are realising that if they don't give up the drugs or alcohol they will lose their family, their children, all those that love them, and they are understanding how important all of that is.

They are calling out in desperation. They are

praying to God and His angels not to give up on them, not to allow their family to give up on them either.

They are recognising, through this prayer, that they cannot do it on their own, but they are now ready to try. They are prepared to give up the drugs or the alcohol. They are going to fight with all the strength they have, but they need encouragement from those whom they love, although they may have hurt them terribly and even tried to destroy them.

Knowing that they are loved by their family and friends gives a drug addict encouragement to give up the drugs and alcohol, to set themselves free, to get their life back again. It is important to know that every day. They have to take one day at a time surrounded by their loved ones.

Prayer from a Drug Addict's or Alcoholic's Mother

Dear God,
I am a mother,
And my child has completely lost their way.
They got involved with the wrong crowd,
And now my child is a drug addict/alcoholic.
My heart is torn apart.

I've done everything possible to help my child.
My child turned my help away,
And gave me abuse, stole from me, and even
hit me.
God, I hear your words.
I hear what my guardian angel is whispering
to me,
That I must be strong.
God, please give me the strength to be there
for my child,
Even in the shadows.
Keep your angels on guard
Because my child thinks I am the enemy
Because of the drugs/alcohol,
And turns away all the help.
Just knowing you are there, my God,
Is giving me the strength.
Thank you for my guardian angel
Guiding me to help my child.
Amen.

This is a parent in desperation, it could be a mother or a father, crying out to God, seeing their child being desolated by drugs or alcohol. They are feeling completely helpless, because their child locks onto them as the enemy, but the parents are only trying to help; to save their child, no matter what abuse or violence the child gives them. These parents are doing their best not to give up on their child, because they love them, and are asking for God's help to give them the strength they will need on this journey.

They are so terrified that one day someone will knock on the door and tell them that their child has died from an overdose, or from alcohol poisoning, or from some kind of violence on the street. No parent wants this for their child, because each parent sees all the good in their child, all the love that is there, even though it has been overcome by drugs and alcohol.

These parents are reaching out to their child with a helping hand. They are stretching out their hands as far as they can, asking the child to take it for the right reasons, to give up the drugs and alcohol. They want to help set their child free again, for the child to take back their life.

No parent wants to watch their child die from drugs, alcohol or disease, to hear that they have been knifed in a fight over drugs and have died. It is a parent's nightmare, and a shocking experience for all the family.

Prayer for a Sibling

Dear God,

I implore all of your angels to surround my sibling.

They are doing something I know they shouldn't be doing, God.

I am scared for him/her.

I asked my guardian angel to ask their guardian angel to get my sibling to listen,

To stop doing what he's doing.

Keep your angels encircling him, to never give up on him, my God.

Amen.

I love this prayer. I often receive letters from young teenagers asking me to pray for their brother or sister, usually because they are doing drugs, or drinking a huge amount of alcohol, and doing very dangerous things that might hurt them or others, and the teenager is very scared. Many times, they ask their brother or sister about what is going on and their sibling gets very angry with them in response and threatens them; so they send me a letter, asking for me to pray to God for their brother or sister but, in their asking, they are praying themselves as well.

You could be a teenager, or even younger, or someone of an older age, imploring God to have their brother or sister surrounded by angels, because they know their sibling is doing something wrong. They have so much love for them and they want the best for them, and in this prayer they are telling God all of this.

They have asked their guardian angel to ask their sibling's guardian angel for help. They simply want their sibling to stop doing what they are doing and are asking God to keep all those beautiful angels encircling their brother or sister, and never to give up on them, because they won't give up on their brother or sister either.

Many of us, no matter what age we are, are often scared for those we love, especially when we see someone that we care for going down the wrong road in life. You do everything possible to help them, but it is never easy. In our hearts, we know that prayer helps to give us strength to help those we love. Do not forget to pray.

CHAPTER TEN

Prayers for Healing in Yourself and Others

Prayer for a Loved One's Surgery

Dear God,
Send all your Healing Angels
To surround my loved one who is having heart
*   surgery.*
Have your Healing Angels guide the hands of
*   the surgeon.*
Pour your loving grace down upon my loved one.
Please God, let it be a success.
Amen.

YOU ARE ASKING GOD IN THIS PRAYER TO GUIDE THE HANDS of the surgeon, for the Healing Angels to be present there, and for God to pour out more of His loving grace upon your loved one to give them the strength they need for the surgery they are having. You are asking God for the surgery to be a success.

This is a prayer anyone can say, and I know there are other prayers that are being said all around the world, including the Prayer of Thy Healing Angels, which is at the beginning of this book. It is a powerful prayer. When someone is going for surgery, no matter what kind of surgery it is, we should always say lots of prayers. Every prayer counts.

Prayer for My Child's Heart Surgery

Dear God,
You hold my little loved one in the palm of
*   your hands.*
They are so small.
They need heart surgery and I need you, my
*   God. Cradle them close to your heart,*
Fill them with your healing grace.
God, my little one is in your hands.
Send your healing light, your love, my God,
For my little one to grow strong.

This I ask of you, my God.
Amen.

This prayer could be from a mother and father, coming from their heart. They know everything is in God's hands. They are asking God to allow the surgery of their baby or young child to be successful, so that their child can grow up to do all the normal things that every other healthy child does.

I hear from many parents all over the world. They are always asking me to write a prayer for their child who is having heart surgery. This is only one prayer, but there are many that could be said.

Prayer for My Child's Surgery

Dear God,
Through my tears, I am begging you,
My God, to allow the surgery that
My child is going through to be successful.
My child's life is in your hands, my God.
I promise you, my God, and all of the angels
*   of the heavens that*
I will be the best parent I possibly can be.
I won't let you down, my God.
Amen.

This is the prayer of a parent opening their heart to God, knowing that the life of their child is in God's hands, and not just the hands of the doctors and surgeons. They have great faith and belief that there is a chance their child will live and the surgery will be successful. They keep hope burning in their hearts that their child will grow healthy and strong, and that they will hear their child's laughter and see their child playing again. They want to see them grow up into a teenager, to become a young adult, possibly a parent. They are asking God for a future for their child.

For a child to be ill is the worst possible time for all parents and for their family. To watch a child suffering is unimaginable for those who have never had a sick child within the family. A parent feels so helpless and every parent wishes that they could take on the pain instead of their child, or that God would give them the disease or the sickness, so their child is no longer suffering. Even in prayer, parents ask for this.

Many parents say to me, 'Where is God when a child is suffering like this?'

I don't have an answer. I don't believe there is an answer to this in the way we would like to understand. Our human bodies are not perfect.

Why does a little soul choose its parents and come all the way from heaven to be conceived, while knowing all the while it will have a certain disease that will cause great pain and suffering, and soon die?

Those little children know before they are conceived how long they are going to stay on Earth and when they are going home to heaven or, indeed, get better and grow up to have a family of their own. They still choose to be born, and for you to be their parents, their mum and dad, and they love you unconditionally. They knew that you would love and care for them. They chose you.

These little babies give lots of love to their parents, their family and all those around them.

Here are a few prayers that I have been given. They are very simple, so anyone can say them. I hope you do.

Prayer for Pregnancy

Dear God,
Assemble your special angels
For I am beginning to lose hope
Of having a child of my own.
I am praying to you, my God.
I am asking my guardian angel to speak to
    you on my behalf.
I have faith, and I believe you will answer my
    prayer.
God, assemble your angels,

Guide them with a little soul to come to me.
Allow me to become pregnant.
I implore you, my God and all your angels.
Amen.

This could be any couple in the world having difficulties conceiving and praying to God and the angels to
send a soul, a little baby, to them. They want to hold
a child in their arms. They want to be a mother and
father. There are many couples all over the world who
are having difficulties becoming pregnant. This is
something I predicted in *Stairways to Heaven*, a future
that the angels showed to me and has since become a
crisis. This is a prayer coming from a couple's hearts
in desperation, asking God to assemble His angels to
guide the soul of their little baby to them.

This prayer shows a mother wanting to carry her
own little baby in her tummy, wanting to feel the baby
as it grows, feel the kicks and all the ups and downs
she would go through, and to give birth to her own
child. The father wants the same, but in a different
way; to help his partner through the pregnancy, and
to be there holding her hand for the birth. He wants
to hold his child for the first time in his arms, to
provide all the love he can to the little baby God sends,
and to take care of and love their child.

Most importantly, they want to be the best parents they can possibly be, giving their child all the love that they can.

Prayer to Mary for Safe Birth

Hail Mary, full of grace,
I beseech you, hear my prayer,
Pour your loving grace down upon me
For I am with child.
Holy Mary, my Mother, keep my baby safe.
Let my child be born safely,
Just as your son, Jesus, was born.
Mary, my Mother.
I love you.
Amen.

This is from a woman who is about to become a mother. The mother saying the prayer is telling Mary that she is feeling excited about the child that is growing inside her, but she is also afraid of something going wrong. This mother is asking Our Queen Mother Mary to keep her baby safe and pour her grace down upon them.

The mother remembers the story of Mary and Joseph, when Mary was pregnant with baby Jesus, and the happiness and joy that Mary felt, just as this mother is feeling, but also the nervousness and fear that something might go wrong. She is asking Our Lady, our Queen Mother in heaven, to keep her baby safe, for her to hold her baby in her arms. It is a lovely prayer.

Prayer for Pain

Dear God, I thank you for everything you have given me in this life,
But I am in such pain. Now I ask you,
God, to send your Healing Angels to help to ease my pain.
Thank you, my God.
Amen.

This is a general prayer of someone suffering, when the physical body is in constant pain and it won't go away. This is a prayer I have often been asked for. Over the years, I have heard from many people: men and women, young and old, even children, who say they are in constant pain for one reason or another, sometimes for all of their life. Some of them have been in pain for many years, and others for a shorter period of time.

I know as we grow older, our bodies often begin to feel more pain. Some of us seem to have more pain than others. I am always asking God to ease the pain in people's bodies, especially when they have grown old.

Prayer for Arthritis

My dearest guardian angel,
Please implore God and all of His angels
About this pain of mine.
I thank God for the wonderful life He had
  given me.
Please, my guardian angel,
I am asking for a miracle, for my arthritis not
  to pain so much.
Thank you.
Amen.

Many people around the world ask me to pray for the pain that is in the body, because they have arthritis. Sometimes we can underestimate the pain of arthritis. This prayer is a way of asking your guardian angel to implore God on your behalf for a miracle for you, even if it only eases the pain of your arthritis. It is a horrific disease. Always ask God for a miracle, but do what you can to keep your body as healthy as possible.

Prayer to Help Me Walk Again

Dear God,
Pour your grace of hope upon me.
Help me to walk again.

> *Lay your healing hand upon my head, my*
>   *God.*
> *Instil within me, my God,*
> *The strength to walk again.*
> *Have your angels help me not to give up.*
> *Have them by my side, helping me to walk.*
> *I thank you, God, for everything.*
> *Amen.*

I have met many people who have ended up in wheel-chairs through car crashes, or sometimes through illness. They need great strength and comfort. In this prayer, they are asking God to give them that strength, and to help them walk again, if that is possible. I know that sometimes it is not possible, because the injuries are too extensive. Even if they are not as bad as this, it still takes great strength and it is such a struggle.

They can put one foot in front of the other, but it usually causes great pain and a huge amount of energy for a person to get to that point, for them to walk again. However, I know many people who have walked again, so don't give up. Ask God and your guardian angel to help you. I am always asking for miracles for people to walk again. It is one thing I will end up asking for at a blessing, but the individuals themselves have to work very hard with their physical body and with their minds.

Prayer for Sleeping

My guardian angel,
Before I go to sleep,
Shield and protect me with your wings.
Wrap your arms tightly around me.
Let my soul give praise and thanks to God
*   while I sleep.*
Amen.

This is a prayer that I say personally myself. It is a prayer that the Angel Amen taught me when she would sit on my bed with me in Old Kilmainham, which was our home and my father's old bicycle shop in Dublin. Well, it wasn't exactly a shop. I suppose my dad just repaired bicycles. I have said this prayer ever since. To me, it's a very special prayer.

Within this prayer, I am asking God to allow my soul to continue praying while my human body sleeps. I would give praise and thanks as a child for everything that happened to me that day, but that has changed. Now, I give praise and thanks for everything from the moment of my birth to this very day; thanks not only for myself, but for all of us in the world.

CHAPTER ELEVEN

Our Lady Mary and Prayer

Prayer for the Prayer Scroll

Archangel Michael,
I have the prayer scroll in my hand.
Archangel Michael,
Take my soul, guide me to the Throne of Heaven.
God, my Father, I kneel before you with an
 outstretched hand.
Let the healing begin, whatever way you, my
 God, my heavenly Father, grants it,
I beseech you for all of the names of your
 children on the prayer scroll.

Please, my Lord and my God, help them.
Amen.

THIS IS A PRAYER I HAVE BEEN ALLOWED TO SHARE WITH you. I can only share some of its words, not all of the words, that I speak to God when I bring the prayer scroll and kneel at His feet.

I call on the Archangel Michael almost every day. But, if there is a day I forget, the Archangel Michael comes anyway, and he takes my soul to heaven. We walk hand in hand towards the Throne of God. All the time, I carry the prayer scroll in my right hand and the Archangel Michael holds my left.

Again, I am a child going to see my Father and I am full of excitement and joy. My soul cannot stay still. I cannot find the words to explain, but from the moment Archangel Michael takes my soul to heaven, I feel that overpowering love of God. Even though the Archangel Michael holds my hand, I still want to run and hide, because God's love is so pure and I am not sure what expression to use . . . it takes my breath away.

I kneel at the feet of God and stretch out my hand while talking to Him. God stretches out His hand and takes the prayer scroll and opens it. It always seems so long, never-ending, and God smiles at me. I cannot share with you what we talk about, at the moment anyway. Maybe someday I can share more of the prayer that I say to God.

Prayer to Our Heavenly Mother

Mary, my Queen Mother in heaven, be by my
  side,
Shield me with your grace of loving light,
Always guiding and protecting me.
Mary, my mother, I love you.
Amen.

This is a beautiful short prayer to Our Lady, your mother and mine, and the mother of Our Lord Jesus Christ, asking for protection and for guidance. It reminds our Queen Mother Mary, Our Lady, that we love her.

Prayer to Mary for Peace in the World

Hail Mary, Queen of the Heavens,
Mother, Queen of All Mankind.
I beseech you to intercede with your son, Our
  Lord, Jesus Christ
On behalf of mankind, for peace in the world.
Mary, my mother.
I love you.
Amen.

This is another prayer to Our Lady, Queen of Heaven, the Queen of All Mankind, asking her to intercede with her son, Our Lord, Jesus Christ, on behalf of us all. Regardless of our differences or beliefs, you are asking Our Lady, the Mother of God, to ask her son to help us all to bring peace into the world. It is a simple and short prayer, and easy enough to say.

Prayer to Mary for Guidance

Hail Mary, Mother of God,
Queen of Angels,
Queen of Humankind,
Mary, our Heavenly Mother,
Mentor of all your children.
Protect us and guide us on our journey through
*   life.*
Mary, Mother of Jesus.
I love you.
Amen.

We are reminded in this prayer of who Mary is. Many of us have forgotten, and we all need her help because of who she is. She is the Queen Mother, your Mother, my Mother, Queen of all the Angels, the Queen of the Human Race. Most importantly, she is the mother of Our Lord, Jesus Christ, and she is a great example, a mentor to all of us. We are asking for protection and guidance during our journey through our lives.

Prayer to Mary for Encouragement to Pray

Hail Mary,
Mother of Our Lord, Jesus Christ,
You give messages to us all,
All of the time to pray,
But we are not listening.
Mary, Queen Mother of Heaven, help us to
pray more.
Mary, Mother of Jesus,
I love you.
Amen.

Our Lady has been telling the world to pray, and how important prayer is, and that we should pray every day for ourselves and our families. In fact, we need to pray for everyone in the world, for peace to come to us all, but sadly many of us are not listening to this message. We are ignoring it, because we are caught up in ourselves so much, in our own lives, that we feel we don't have time to pray.

Prayer takes only a moment. You could be on your lunch break during work. Even sitting at a table, or if you are out walking, you can say a quick prayer.

No matter what you are doing or what is happening in your life, you always have time to pray. We need to pray for each other. We need to pray for our world to change for us all. Regardless of our religion or our differences, we all need to pray for each other to make this world a better place.

Our Lady has been asking for all of us to pray, so I am asking you now – please pray.

Prayer to Have Peace

My dearest guardian angel,
I thank God for everything in my life
But for a long time now, I have had no peace.
I am ready now to be still and quiet, to listen
*   to God*
To have peace,
To take time out now and be silent for a few
*   minutes.*
Thank you for helping me to have peace.
Amen.

This prayer is relevant at different times in our lives. We all want to have peace. But from time to time I find it hard to even understand those words myself. When God gave me this prayer, He didn't say it was a prayer for peace of mind, or peace within the family or country. He just said this prayer is to have peace, so I can't change the words. I guess anyone who says this prayer will understand what those three words mean to themselves and no one else.

I guess that is why this prayer is special in that way for each individual personally and to no one else. Don't forget to be silent and take those few minutes to be quiet and allow yourself to have peace.

Prayer for Truth

My dearest guardian angel,
Please ask God to forgive me
For I find it very hard to be truthful. It's easier
*   to lie than to speak the truth.*
My lies hurt others and myself. I never seem
*   to learn my lesson.*
Please ask God to help me to listen to you,
*   my guardian angel.*
Help me to be still and quiet.
Amen.

If you can, take a moment and be still.

God, I know I'm ready now. I am listening.
Now, I hesitate hearing my guardian angel,
*   and I don't lie.*

Thank you for helping me.
Amen.

Sometimes we need to take time to think about the prayer we say. Prayer is very powerful. It is one of the strongest forces in the world, like love, but it is good to learn how to allow a prayer to penetrate our mind and body, to become deeply attached to the prayer, so that we can listen and hear. When you are in prayer, and are aware of your soul coming forward, your soul can come back into your body and bring prayer with it. Your soul can then move forward again and let prayer out.

I have often asked for this to happen, so that I can put more of my soul into the prayer to enhance it more. I do this without words, but it might be helpful for you to ask God for this. I usually do this when I feel close to tears for all the bad that is happening in the world, especially when I see us not going in the right direction. This helps us to turn in the right direction. It gives me great hope. When you do this your whole being, not just your soul, is praying.

Allow the prayer to touch your soul; pray with every part of your being. This is a prayer to help you not to lie, but instead to speak the truth, for we all find it easier to lie now and then, even though that always makes life more complicated and causes problems in the end.

Speaking the truth makes life easier. It makes you happier as well. Always do your best to listen to your guardian angel. Your guardian angel is telling you not to say what you are thinking. If it is wrong, your guardian angel will give you that guilty feeling, and you know, deep down inside of you, that you are not being truthful. Don't ignore your guardian angel – listen.

Prayer to Follow God

God,
I adore you and love you.
Have your angels each side of me, in front of
me and behind me,
Guiding me so I follow you, God,
With goodness and love in my heart at all
times.
Your radiant light shining before me.
I love you and adore you, my God.
Amen.

This is a little prayer that I say myself. The Angels of Prayer say this prayer with me every now and then. I repeat the words they say, and sometimes we say the prayer in rhythm. This prayer allows me to tell God that I love Him and adore Him, and I am asking Him to have His angels each side of me all the time. From time to time the words change a little; I think this is because of what is going on in the world.

Prayer for God to Set Me Free

My God,
You are my refuge, my strength, and without
  you, I can do nothing.
God, set me free from all the temptations that
  surround me every day.
Pour your angels down from the heavens.
Have your light encircle me.
Let the light of your love, my God,
Dissolve all the chains of temptation.
Set me free, my God, with your love, peace,
  hope and compassion.
Amen.

This prayer is asking God to set you free from all the chains of negativity in your life; all of those temptations that you know you don't want. It can be as simple as acting out in jealousy or talking badly about another person. I know we all need to say this prayer every now and then throughout our lives to be set free. Instead, we need to be filled with the peace and hope that come from God's love and compassion, because when you are set free and release all that negativity, you find peace within yourself.

You are not afraid any more, because you know God's love is right there with you, and all His angels are there, too. It is a freedom that each and every one of us has to discover for ourselves, and at different times in our lives we will feel that freedom. It is a beautiful prayer.

Prayer to Archangel Michael

Archangel Michael,
I implore you to ask God
To allow you to pierce the hearts of everyone
    in the world.
Archangel Michael, with your mighty sword
Bestow on us goodwill towards everyone;
For the tip of your sword to evaporate hatred,
    anger, and revenge;
For goodwill to blossom in our world; for all
    our hearts to be filled with love and peace.
Thank you, Archangel Michael. Thank you,
    my God.
Amen.

You are praying to God through Archangel Michael in this prayer. The Archangel Michael is an extremely powerful angel. He is at the Throne of God and yet he is also with each and every one of us when we call on him. This is a special prayer that the Archangel Michael has asked me to share with you. I have said this prayer with the Archangel Michael on many occasions and hopefully I ask you to say this prayer too, so that when the Archangel Michael pierces your heart with the tip of his sword, you will start to feel goodwill towards mankind and your fellow neighbours, and you will lose any hatred, anger and want for revenge inside of you.

Archangel Michael works very hard defending us all the time. He has given me this prayer and has asked you to say it, but it is not for Archangel Michael. It is for you, for all of us, if each and every one of us accepted Archangel Michael piercing our hearts with his sword and filling us with love and hope. Archangel Michael is showing you that we can do it. We can have a peaceful and wonderful world. We can live in harmony with each other. When you say this prayer, Archangel Michael is saying it with you.

Prayer to Help Me to Get Closer to God

Dear God,
I ask you for your divine help.
I long to get closer to you.
Let my soul shine radiantly as it longs to get
*   closer to you, my God.*
Let you, my God, be always on my mind.
Let me give you praise and thanks every
*   moment of my life.*
Allow me to come closer to you, my God,
For my soul and heart longs for this.
I love you, my God.
Amen.

This prayer is about asking God to allow you to become closer to Him. Prayer is one of the most powerful ways to get closer to God and this is a prayer that will help you. It is reminding you to pray, and to feel the love that is in your soul and your heart. The more you pray, the more peaceful and happy you feel, because you are getting in touch with God. You are getting closer to God. You are allowing your soul to shine, to be radiant. Allow yourself to feel your pure love as your soul gets closer to God.

Prayer for Forgiveness for
Those Who Have Hurt Me

Dear God,
Please forgive those that have hurt me
Because I forgive them.
Amen.

This is another prayer that I have said since I was a child. Maybe one day I will tell you the full story, but not today. In this little prayer, you are opening your heart and sending love towards the person who has hurt you, because you have forgiven them. They are powerful words. You are asking God to forgive those who have hurt you, because you have forgiven them. I say this prayer every day. You might ask why I would need to say this prayer, but I say it every day because God told me to do so.

Even though this is a short prayer, it is a very powerful prayer.

CHAPTER TWELVE

God's Belief in You

Prayer to Set Me Free

Dear God,
Have your archangels surround me with their
shields.
Let your angels break the chains that hold me
down.
Let me see the light shimmer from the shields
of your archangels,
Hear the rattles of the chains as they fall from
me.
Let me rush forward towards the light,

Knowing I am free now to live my life
That you have given me, my God,
For I could not have done it without you.
Thank you. I love you, my God.
Amen.

THIS IS ANOTHER PRAYER ABOUT FREEING YOURSELF IN EVERY aspect of your life and moving forward. It is about releasing the chains that have held you down and have stopped you from living your life. The angels are helping you to break free of those chains and the archangels are surrounding you with their shields, so that you can see their light. Know that you could not have done it without God's help, because it took all your strength, courage and confidence. You listened to your guardian angel and your friends, who were told to give you courage and confidence. They listened, too, and they helped you to free yourself.

We always need help to free ourselves in our lives at different times. Sometimes we allow ourselves to be locked away because we are so scared of life, but we shouldn't be, as life is wonderful.

In this prayer, you are calling on God, the archangels and all the angels to set you free, but you have to do it as well. If you feel chains are holding you down, say this prayer to help you set yourself free.

Prayer for When You Can't Do Everything Alone

Dear God,
I thank you, God, for my life.
I can't do everything alone.
I need to know, my God,
That I have a guardian angel.
Grant a sign for me, my God, no matter how
small.
I love you, my God.
Amen.

This prayer is about realising that you can't do everything alone. In this prayer, you are asking God to give you a sign to show that you have a guardian angel, who is with you all the time.

God and the angels, your guardian angel, and your loved ones that have gone home to heaven, are sending you help every day. Sometimes we find it hard to ask for help or to take it when it is offered. We should all offer help to each other more often than we do, so that no one feels they have to do everything on their own.

In this prayer, you are reminding God that you can't do everything alone. When Jesus walked the earth, he didn't do everything on his own. He had the apostles, his mother and father, all his friends and all of the people who came to see him, so he never did anything alone. Of course, he was surrounded by the angels and his own guardian angel.

Prayer for My Guardian Angel's Help When I Feel Down

My guardian angel,
When I feel down for any reason at all,
I talk to you, my guardian angel,
As I would a close friend.
When I do this, I hear my angel's reassurance
and guidance.
Thank you, guardian angel, for listening to
my worries.
Amen.

It should be as natural talking to your guardian angel as if to a friend. You can share all your troubles and all your secrets with your guardian angel. This is something you should do every day, and that is what this prayer is doing. It is reminding you that your guardian angel is your best friend, actually beyond your best friend, because it is connected to you in a way that no human being could ever be. Your guardian angel loves you to talk, to share your secrets, to share your troubles and your worries – everything that is on your mind – because your guardian angel won't judge you in any way.

Your guardian angel will respond to you by helping you feel that a huge load has been lifted off your shoulders, and how wonderful it is to share everything with your guardian angel. At that moment, you start to feel the reassurance of your guardian angel being right there with you. You know you are not alone. Then you start to understand the guidance your guardian angel is giving you.

Your guardian angel can help in two ways: by lightening the burden and by giving you advice.

This prayer is a wonderful prayer. It is one you can say even while you are sitting on a bus, in a taxi, or on a plane; simply start talking to your guardian angel in your mind, as if your guardian angel is sitting in the seat beside you, or in front of you. Share everything with your guardian angel.

Prayer of Thanks for Blessings

Dear God,
Thank you for all the blessings you have
bestowed upon me, my God.
The blessing of having a soul, that spark of
your light,

> *The blessing of the gift of my guardian angel*
> *for eternity,*
> *That never leaves me, not even for one second,*
> *The blessing of the peace and love that dwells*
> *in me,*
> *The blessing of my family that you have given*
> *me,*
> *The blessing of those you sent into my life for*
> *companionship,*
> *The blessing of living in harmony with those*
> *around me,*
> *The blessing of my labour, my work,*
> *The blessing of all the material things I have*
> *in my life, big and small,*
> *The blessing of this wonderful world and the*
> *nature around me.*
> *Thank you, my God, for all the things I've*
> *forgotten to thank you for,*
> *And most of all, thank you, my God, for*
> *continuing to bless my life.*
> *Amen.*

This is a prayer that I wrote many years ago. It is in my book *A Message of Hope from the Angels*. It is a prayer of thanksgiving for all our blessings. Each and every one of us has so many blessings in our lives that if I had continued to write that prayer, it would have been so long it would not have fitted into the book. That's why at the end of the prayer, I thank God for the blessings I forgot to mention. If anything comes to mind when you are saying this prayer, you can mention it as well.

Just look around you, look at each day of your life and you will see the blessings you have in your life. There are so many blessings that we take for granted. We don't even think about them until they are taken away. Many of us will have a blessing taken away abruptly.

One of those blessings that can be taken away from us, slowly over time, is our ability to see. For lots of us, our eyes fail as we grow older. Some of us lose our eyesight completely. It is only when our sight has gone that we realise what a blessing it was to be able to see.

Prayer for Friends

God,
I thank you for the friends you have given me.
Shield them and keep them safe;
To always be friends and not to fall out;
To be there for each other and to allow new
    friends in.

Allow the light of your angels to always shine
around my friends.
Thank you, my God.
Amen.

This short prayer is about recognising how precious it is to have friends in your life. In this prayer you are asking that you never fall out with your friends and that you will be there for each other throughout your life. You are asking God to shield them, to protect them and keep them safe. You are asking for the light of His angels to shine around them. We should always say prayers for our friends.

Prayer for When You Have No Friends

Dear God,
I asked my guardian angel to help me to make
a friend.
My guardian angel is helping me,
But I'm very shy so I ask you, my God,
Send more angels from heaven to give me
courage and confidence.
I am so lonely. I need a friend.
I cannot do this without your help.
Thank you, my God.
Amen.

This prayer represents hundreds of thousands of people across the world, maybe millions, who have no friends, not even one. Usually they are very shy and afraid to go out, or to have a short conversation, even to say hello to someone. Some actually lock themselves away in a room – away from the world.

I often hear from parents who are so worried for the young members of their family. I hear from the mother or father that their son or daughter doesn't have one friend, because they are so shy. If they are asked to go somewhere, they say no.

This prayer is for someone who wants to change. It is for someone who wants to ask God and their guardian angel to help them to make friends. Even one friend would be wonderful, and they are asking God to send extra angels to help them to have confidence and courage.

So if you are one of these people who will make the effort, you will find a friend, because there is someone else out there looking for a friend, too. Remember, parents can say this prayer for their child.

Prayer to Save Souls

Jesus, Mary, I love you.
Save souls.
Amen.

This is a prayer that the angels taught me when I was a very young child. I smiled one day when my grandmother at her hostel in Mount Shannon, Co. Clare, repeated this prayer to me, for I never knew anyone else had heard of the prayer. The angels just smiled at me.

This prayer is in my book *Angels in My Hair*, but a word was added that is not meant to be there. Things like that can happen at times, that is why Angel Hosus said this prayer was to go into this prayer book, so that people will recognise it is a prayer, not just words.

This prayer is to save the souls of the living. It is to help the intertwining of our body and soul. It is not about saving souls from going to hell. It goes beyond that. It is to save us all from taking a wrong turn for humankind. I believe we can choose to go the right way.

Prayer to Accept God's Love

Dear God,
I wish to surrender to your love.
Allow your love, my God, to dwell inside of me,
Allow your divine presence to grow within me,
Allow your grace, my God, to destroy my
*   denial of your love.*
Touch my heart, my God, and surround me
*   with your angels.*
Thank you, my God,
Amen.

This is a short prayer of the longing to surrender to God's love. It is about allowing that love to dwell inside of you. It will help to destroy the denial of God's love that has been in your life all the time, even though you did not always see it, but now you have grown older and you want to become closer to God, your guardian angel and all His angels.

Prayer for Thanking God

My Heavenly Father,
Thank you for being my Father, for watching
*   over and protecting me,*
For loving me when I was good,

But most importantly, for loving me when I
  was bad.
Thank you, my Heavenly Father, for loving
  me, just as I am.
Amen.

This is a prayer thanking God, our Heavenly Father, for loving us as we are, good or bad. It is a very powerful prayer to say when you have been doing good things in your life, when you have been loving, kind, compassionate and helping others.

Importantly, it is also a prayer to say in times when you have not been so good, when maybe you have been angry and have not been loving or compassionate. Knowing that God loves you, this prayer gives you the hope that you can start all over again and do your best to be a good, loving, caring person.

Prayer to Call on Archangel Michael

Archangel Michael, I call on you;
Be by my side today
For I am weak and vulnerable.
Surround me with your shield of protection.
Give me strength and comfort.
Thank you, Archangel Michael.
Amen.

Prayer of Thanks

Dear God,
I thank God for me,
And for you, Archangel Michael.
Amen.

This is a short prayer thanking God from yourself and for the Archangel Michael being in your life. You are thanking God for this wonderful angel, who has done so much for our world and has helped many people by interceding with God for us all.

Prayer for the Gift from Heaven

Dear God,
I beseech you, my God, instil within us the
    power of prayer,
That never-ending powerful force that comes
    from heaven.
Place it within that radiant spark of light, our
    soul.
I love you, God.
Amen.

This prayer is about accepting within ourselves the powerful force of prayer that comes from heaven. The powerful force of prayer resides in heaven, it is

God itself. We are praying for what we need humanly in this world, as well as what we need spiritually. The force comes down, we personalise it and send it back up.

The powerful force of prayer that comes from heaven becomes part of us, because of the connection with our soul, which then informs that force.

Our soul is that spark of light of God within every one of us and, if we allow it, our soul can be in constant prayer. There can be a stream of prayer all the time from each and every one of us to the heavens, to the Throne of God. Imagine how that powerful force of prayer could be manifested in the future, how it could change our world, how it could heal everything. Most of us are shown the power of prayer at various times in our lives. I am sure that if we all prayed, we could actually move mountains.

Today, I believe it is easier for us to learn how to pray, because we are all so much more knowledgeable about the spiritual side of ourselves, our soul. We make decisions to pray, or to meditate, in so many different ways. Nowadays we have the freedom to make these choices. We don't have to stick to ancient rituals handed down from our forefathers.

We also know we can pray anywhere, although we still love to pray in sacred, holy places, because we feel the sense of the peace and spirituality there. We have allowed ourselves to be free to pray.

Prayer for God to Believe in Me

Dear God,
Believe in me, God,
So I can believe in myself.
Without you, my God, I am nothing
For I can do nothing on my own, my God,
   without your help.
Your belief in me, my God, is all I have.
It helps me believe in myself.
You, my God, are my refuge and my strength.
Thank you, God.
Amen.

This prayer asks God to believe in you, so that you can believe in yourself. You are reaching out to God and hoping that He believes in you, even though deep down you know that God does. This helps you to believe in yourself. This is about God showing you within yourself that He believes in you. You will experience and feel this belief. I think this is a prayer we all need to say at certain times in our life, especially when we lose faith, when we are at rock bottom.

At these times, we realise that we need to know

that God believes in us. We recognise that without God's help and the help of Our Lady, and all the angels and our guardian angel, we are not going to make it. It is so important that we are all aware of God, Our Lady, all of God's angels, our loved ones, and all the saints that have gone home to heaven.

CHAPTER THIRTEEN

Our Soul and Our Spiritual Journey

Prayer to Thank God for My Guardian Angel

Dear God,

Thank you for the precious gift of my guardian angel which

Never leaves me for one second,

Who guides and protects me,

And loves me unconditionally with love never-ending,

And never gives up on me

Even if others do,

With its loving arms around me all the time,
Never to let me go.
Thank you, God, for the most wonderful gift
  of all: my guardian angel.
Amen.

GOD HAS ME WRITING MANY PRAYERS THAT YOU CAN SAY to your guardian angel. All the words that have been given to me for each and every prayer in this prayer book have come from God. God wants each prayer within the book to touch your heart and your soul, to help you learn how to pray. I love the words of this prayer, as it thanks God for my guardian angel, whom I know loves me unconditionally with a love that is never-ending. Even if others give up on you, I know your guardian angel will not give up on you.

Prayer to Ask for Guardian Angels to Help with Everyday Tasks

My dear guardian angel,
Help me to accomplish what I need to do
  today.
The tasks are small, but they are enormous
  to me.
If you could ask God maybe to send some
  extra angels to help.

> *I don't want to bother God too much, my*
> *   guardian angel.*
> *Thank you, my guardian angel, for helping*
> *   me to accomplish my tasks today.*
> *Amen.*

This is a prayer to your guardian angel, asking for help to accomplish the things you need to do each day. It asks your guardian angel to ask God for extra help from some other angels as well. Talk to your guardian angel in prayer as you would your best friend. To me this is a lovely prayer. I am always asking my guardian angel to help me to accomplish everything I need each day. You can do this, too, just say this prayer.

Prayer for the Daily Grind

> *Dear God,*
> *I need your help to help me to get through*
> *   this day.*
> *I hate my job.*
> *I find it tough and hard.*
> *It does not really interest me.*
> *I find it boring and it makes me tired.*
> *Help me to see the positive in what I do*
> *So it won't feel like a daily grind*

And for things to change for the good.
Thank you, my God,
Amen.

Most of us, at some time in our lives, end up doing something we have no interest in and we find completely boring. This is a prayer helping you to change that, so that one day in the future you will be doing something you love and it will not be a daily grind.

Prayer for When God Touches My Soul

Dear God,
Thank you, my God, for you touched my soul,
And with tears of relief, my God, you allowed
    such calmness within
Of love and hope.
Thank you, my God.
Amen.

This is a powerful prayer. When God touches your soul, His love gives you hope and relief. It brings such calmness and peace. This often happens to people in times of enormous stress, tragedy and hopelessness. When in prayer and crying out to God, He touches your soul and gives you such relief that it brings tears to your eyes and you feel a calmness of love and hope.

Prayer for Healing

My guardian angel,
Please pray for me for my healing
So I can go on and live life.
Intercede with God for me
To send his Healing Angels,
So I can live the remainder of my life without
*   too much pain.*
Thank you, my guardian angel, for praying
*   for me.*
Amen.

This is a prayer asking your guardian angel to pray for you and to intercede with God, especially when you need healing within your physical body. You may need healing because of a long-term illness or maybe you are in constant pain because your body has grown old, or you may be feeling low or down within yourself. You are asking your guardian angel to pray for you and to ask God on your behalf to send His Healing Angels.

Prayer for Belonging

Dear God
I implore you, my God,
To send your angels down from Heaven
To help me to find a place where I belong
For I feel I belong nowhere at the moment.
God, you have my guardian angel's arms
  wrapped around me tightly,
Not allowing me to give up on finding a place
  to belong.
Help me to see this place I belong to.
Thank you for helping me, my God.
Amien.

This prayer is especially for someone who feels that they belong nowhere, they don't feel at home anywhere, but we all belong somewhere at different times in our lives. Sometimes we just lose sight of it and this is a prayer asking God to help you to find that place where you belong. It reminds you to feel your guardian angel's arms wrapped tightly around you, not allowing you to give up.

Prayer for Help on My Spiritual Journey

Dear God,
Help me on my spiritual journey.

I am in search of you, my God,
Looking for understanding of the heavens,
Of my soul, my guardian angel, and all your
    angels and the existence of heaven.
I see you walking in front of me, my God,
You are like a radiant light attracting me to
    follow you.
I am thirsty in my search for you, my God.
Thank you for guiding me to find you, my
    God.
Amen.

This is a prayer to give you encouragement for when you are on a spiritual journey to find God and to find understanding of His angels and the heavens. It is a long journey. I believe we start it from the time we are born, and it only ends when our human body dies and our soul goes to heaven with our guardian angel, and we realise that we have been walking with God every day of our lives.

It is because of our soul that we are always in search of God, that we are on a spiritual journey. Regardless of what religion you are, whether you believe in God or not, we keep looking for the meaning of our existence and of all things in nature around us. We are fascinated by it. God fascinates us.

Whether they are scientists or religious philosophers, people go in one direction and another in search of reasons for mankind and how life began. Their theories are forever changing, because science discovers more, and for a time they think they are correct; until something else is found that could alter everything again.

Many of us can only go in search of God through reading spiritual books, like the Bible or the Qur'an, or texts from other religions. I can tell you one thing – God is real, and so is your guardian angel. We all have souls, that speck of light of God, and one day we will meet our loved ones who have passed on, when it is our time to go home to heaven.

Prayer for Refugees

Dear God,
I ask you to help the refugee,
The men, women, children that have to flee
    their own country,
Through no fault of their own
Because of war, poverty, looking for hope.
Help me to have kindness in my heart to help
    them
Because one day, I may be a refugee myself

And it may be a refugee of today
I will be hoping will help me.
So, help me to show kindness and love to the
*   refugee,*
My God,
Amen.

This is a prayer asking for help for refugees. Most of them have nothing. They are ordinary people like you and me. They may speak a different language, or have a different culture, but that is not their fault. We must always reach out and help the stranger.

Again, one day you may need help. I don't believe we help refugees enough. I have met men and women who told me they were refugees, that their parents had fled to another country. They worked hard to raise their families. They are good people.

Prayer for the Everyday Blessings

Dear God,
Thank you for the blessings in my everyday
*   activities.*
Thank you for the blessing of my guardian
*   angel.*
Thank you for the blessing of the unemployed
*   angels who are helping me.*

Thank you for the blessings in my everyday
    life, those that are big and trivial.
Thank you for the blessing of you, my God,
    who are there for me.
Thank you.
Amen.

This is only a short prayer thanking God for the blessings in your everyday activities, whether they are big or trivial, and for your guardian angel and all the unemployed angels that God has put in your life. You are thanking God for the blessing of having God be there for you.

CHAPTER FOURTEEN

Rebuilding Love after Trauma

Prayer for Those Sexually Assaulted

Dear God and my guardian angel,
Please help.
I was sexually assaulted. Please help me to
*   recover.*
I am angry and full of bitterness.
I am completely lost at the moment.
God, my guardian angel and all the Healing
*   Angels,*
I see a little light in the distance,

But my anger and hate keeps putting it out.
Help me to survive and get through this.
God, help me to get my life back, not to be
full of fear.
I need a helping hand, my God.
You know I am a survivor. I will fight to
survive, but it's really hard.
Thank you, God, my guardian angel and all
the Healing Angels for your help.
Amen.

I CAN'T IMAGINE WHAT IT IS LIKE FOR ANYONE WHO HAS been sexually assaulted, but the angels and God have told me it is horrific for that person. It is very hard to pull yourself back together again. This is something terrible that can happen to men, women and children, and sometimes they can be sexually abused for years.

It must completely shatter that person. They must lose all the confidence and belief in themselves and be full of anger and bitterness. This prayer is for someone who has been sexually assaulted. It could be you or someone you love, and you are asking God, your guardian angel and all the Healing Angels to help you, to give you the strength and courage to survive. It is about somehow getting your life back to be as normal as possible.

I know a sexual assault will always stay with you, but God and the angels can work a miracle to help you find the strength to be happy again and to enjoy life. I know you can do it and this prayer will give you strength.

Prayer for Recovering from Sexual Abuse

God,
I give my eternal gratitude to you, my God.
I am free from my fear of the past.
I am free now from the trauma of sexual
  abuse.
Free now to have love and joy in my life.
Thank you, my God,
For everything from this moment on in my
  life.
Amen.

This prayer is for when someone is giving thanks about overcoming sexual abuse. The pain of it, mentally and physically, had stopped them from living a normal life, but now they feel free to have love and joy in their life like everyone else. They are thanking God for their new life from this moment on.

Prayer to be Released from Mental Illness

Dear God,
Release me from my anxiety and depression.
Help me to heal.
Release me from my physical pain.
Release me from my bad habits.
Release me from burdens unknown.
Release me from this horrible place.
Release me to move out of my pain and live
life again.
Let me feel the light of your hope and your
love.
Thank you for helping me, my God.
Amen.

This is a personal prayer for someone who is suffering with anxiety and depression. You are asking God to release you, especially from depression and anxiety, from nervousness and being afraid. You want to move out of the pain, so that you can start to live life again.

I know this prayer will touch many of you personally, because it will be what is happening in your own life or in the life of someone else you know. You can say this prayer for them as well, especially if they cannot see it for themselves.

I hope you do say this prayer for someone you know.

It could be a family member or a friend, or even someone you don't know but you have heard they are suffering from the pain of anxiety and depression, or any type of mental illness.

Prayer for Sunshine and Joy in Life

Thank you, God,
For another day of sunshine and joy in my
*   life.*
God, could you grant that the rest of my days
*   that*
I have left to be filled with sunshine and joy.
Thank you for every day
I have left, my God.
Amen.

This is a prayer said by anyone who is dying. Even though it is God's will, they are thanking God for another day of sunshine and enjoyment in life. They are asking God if it would be possible to make the rest of the days of their life full of joy. They are thanking God for every day.

You could even say this prayer for someone whom you know is dying. You can ask that their last days or weeks or months will be full of as much sunshine, joy and love as possible.

Prayer to Heal Relationship Between Parent and Child

My dearest guardian angel,

Help me to have a caring relationship with my child again.

Ask their guardian angel to help them feel love from me.

I love my child very much.

Ask God to surround my child with His angels.

May God bless my child in every way and keep them safe.

Thank you, God.

Amen.

This is a prayer asking for a caring, loving relationship to grow again after it has died between a parent and child. The child may be in their teens, their twenties, forties, or fifties. They could be any age.

This is a parent asking their own guardian angel to ask their child's guardian angel to help. They are asking God to surround their child with His angels to keep them safe, because they love their child. It is hurting them not to have that caring, loving relationship with their child.

Prayer for Teacher Angels

Dear God,
Send as many Teacher Angels
As you possibly can to help my family.
God, we need your Teacher Angels to help us
To be successful in the blessings you have
given us.
Thank you, my God, for your Teacher Angels.
Amen.

You can ask God to send Teacher Angels to help you in any task you need to learn. We know that these are often school exams or study for college, but sometimes it can be for help to learn how to do your new job as best as you possibly can. Maybe it is for help in learning how to ride a bicycle or how to drive a car.

It can be for anything at all that you ask God to send you Teacher Angels to help with your learning. You can ask your guardian angel, too. Your guardian angel cannot allow any other angel in around you unless God says so. I thank God and my guardian angel for having Teacher Angels in and around me when I need them.

Prayer for Exams

Dear God,
Please help me to pass my exam.
I am working as hard as I possibly can.
Help me to have the confidence and belief in
    myself that I can do this.
Thank you, my God,
In advance for helping me.
Amen.

This is a short prayer to help us to pass exams, whether they are for college or for work. We all need help to pass exams, help to have the confidence and belief in ourselves to do the study or work that we need to pass the exams. Ask for the Teacher Angels to be around you, to encourage you to do the work that you need to do, and to help you to listen to them.

Prayer for Hard Times

God,
Pour the grace of hope upon me,
And allow me always to see the light of hope
Burning brightly in front of me.
Light up the darkness by filling me with faith
    and hope

And allow me to receive the comfort of your
   love.
Give me the courage and strength to know
That I will get through these hard times.
Fill me with the joy and trust of knowing
That I am your child, and that you will
Care for me and those I love.
Hear my prayer.
Amen.

This is a prayer for hard times, and we all go through them at different points in our life. Sometimes these hard times may be critical, and at others they are not so bad. No matter what, we will always get through them.

This is a prayer that will help you ask God to pour the grace of hope on you. You are asking to be allowed to see that light of hope burning brightly, lighting up the darkness for you, so that you are able to see a way to get through your difficulties. They may seem enormous, but that light in the darkness is filling you with faith and hope. It gives you the courage and confidence to pick yourself up and stride towards the light of hope. It encourages you to do what you must to help yourself.

God's angels are giving you a helping hand and

giving you joy as well. You know God and all His angels and your guardian angel are going to help you, because you know you are God's child. God cares for you and for those you love. You know that God has heard your prayer.

CHAPTER FIFTEEN

I Am Worthy of God's Love

Prayer of Hope for Christmas

My God,
I ask you this Christmas for the
Gift of the Angel of Hope
To come into my life,
Into the lives of those I love
And into the lives of
Everyone in the world
In need of hope at this time.
Amen.

THIS PRAYER IS FOR THAT SPECIAL TIME OF THE YEAR. YOU are asking God for the gift of the Angel of Hope at Christmas, not only to come into your own life, but into the lives of those whom you love and the lives of everyone around the world that is in need of help, and in need of the gift of the Angel of Hope.

Christmas is a special time to pray, as the gates to heaven are open that little bit more. Similarly around the time of the Spring Equinox, when religions around the world have their special festivals, including Easter and the Passover. I am very aware of history and I am drawn to pray more at these special times of the year.

Prayer for Easter

Dear God,
Forgive me, my God, for the pain and suffering
*   of your son.*
I wish to thank you, my God, for your sacri-
*   fice,*
We would have no resurrection.
Because of this, I know I have life eternally,
That my soul will return to you, my God,
Amen.

Easter is about the crucifixion of God's son, who died for us all, but most importantly it is about the resurrection, about giving us life, freeing us so that our souls will return to God, because God is love.

The only way I can explain it is that on certain days prayers go up to heaven with more force. It is not necessarily the same day every year. They can be quite random. Even if they are not aware, I notice people will start to pray more on those particular days, and they often tell me that they prayed intensely, or for the first time on that day.

I know that from the beginning of November to the New Year, the gates of heaven are open a little bit more. The angels carry more gifts for us, and they also come and gather up any part of a prayer that was in your heart and your soul, but you did not express during your prayers for whatever reason.

Midsummer is a time when we are in prayer and celebrating. At that time there is more joy, but also more fear of not being successful. It is a time of great expectation, but when our greatest hopes are hanging in the balance. It's a time when people feel anxious about whether they are doing the right thing or not, and in this context prayers give guidance, hope and help us become more aware of possibilities and blessings. Prayer helps the midsummer to open up more.

Prayer for Midsummer

Dear God,
Midsummer has arrived, my God,
Thank you for all of the fruits of abundance
  in every aspect of my life
I have now to share with my family and my
  neighbours.
Let the midsummer harvest in their life be as
  good as mine
Or better, if that is possible, my God.
Thank you for the midsummer harvest right
  across the world.
Amen.

Midsummer is about thanking God for the harvest in every aspect of your life, whether it is in your workplace, your family, your friends, or all of nature around you. Everything that you have produced is your midsummer harvest. For each of us has a midsummer harvest of one kind or another in our life, and it is a great thing to acknowledge how well you have done by saying thank you.

The angels often mimic the joy and celebration of

that person and the time of year in a loving way. They are helping to show that there is no need to be anxious or afraid. We should be celebrating.

I often say thank you to God for good things that have happened in the world and what has happened in my family. That is how I praise God by thanking Him. People often feel annoyed when they are told to praise God, because they feel He does not need it. They feel like this because they are not accepting God's love. They haven't stopped to see the blessings, the good things in life.

God does not need our praise in the way we were taught long ago. What He wants is for us to enjoy life as much as possible. When we do that, we are praising Him.

I have written this book because I want us to talk more freely to God, to see God as the person sitting next to us. I want us to pour out our hearts.

Prayer for the Grace of Healing

God,
Thank you, my God, for giving me the grace
of healing.
Help me to become more conscious
Of the power of your healing grace within me,

That powerful force of your love.
Help me to release that healing grace of love
   within me
That comes from my soul
For myself, and those I love and care for.
Amen.

God has given each and every one of us the grace of healing, which dwells inside us all. The grace of healing is a powerful force that comes from our soul. We all have it, because our soul is that speck of light of God, that little piece of Himself that fills every part of us with His grace and light.

We can release this healing grace of love for others and to use for ourselves. We can ask in prayer for this to happen. This asking is part of becoming more aware of your soul and it is especially powerful when your soul comes forward.

I have often seen this healing grace. It is the same force as love. At times, and it depends on the person, I see a different intensity in this healing grace. I think this happens because of where the person is emotionally, psychologically, and physically.

But despite these variations, it always looks so bright. I can't really describe it as having a physical experience. It is radiant. It is so powerful. It is like seeing beyond the light of the sun, like a big explosion that emerges from a person to do its healing work, and then sinks back into them.

We can use this healing grace for ourselves, but we can also use it for others when we pray and when we ask for healing. If a mother or father holds their child when it is crying and the child stops sobbing, it is the grace of healing that the mother or father is using. If you hold the hand of someone when they are in pain and the pain eases, whether it is physical or emotional, it is that gift from God that He has given to every one of us, that grace of healing.

Prayer to See My Self-worth

My beloved God,
Help me to value my self-worth as an indi-
vidual,
To know that I am perfect and unique because
I am your child, my God.
Help me to recognise my own individual
personality.
Help me to believe in myself
To be that person you said I am,
And, most of all, help me to love myself
because I am your child.

With your love, my God, I know I can do this.
Thank you for helping me.
Amen.

This is a prayer for everyone to believe in their self-worth as an individual. It will help you to recognise and know that you are a child of God. It will help you to believe in yourself with positivity and courage. Just being you then brings love, hope, peace and joy. All that happiness comes with acknowledging your own self-worth as an individual.

Prayer for God, You Are My Lifeline

God,
Without you, I could not survive, my God.
You are my lifeline wound tightly around me.
You are my life, my love, my hope. You are
  everything to me
For life would have no meaning to me, my
  God,
Without you, my God, I could never survive
For you give my life meaning, my God.
Amen.

This prayer speaks of the attachment you have to God. It accepts that you could not survive without

God, that He means everything to you. God is your life, and without God it would have no meaning, but because of God your life has the greatest meaning of all. God's love and that little spark of light – your soul – is part of God and His pure love.

Prayer for Luck

God,
I'm praying for a run of luck.
I'm waiting on Jesus to come down from the
*   heavens*
And make everything okay.
I know he will wipe away my tears
And stop the river of pain and hurt
And allow the river of luck to come,
Putting a smile on the faces of those I love.
I thank you, Jesus, in advance for coming
*   down from heaven,*
To tell me everything will be okay.
Thank you, my God.
Amen.

This is a prayer that can be said for so many things. It could be from a husband who has lost his wife. He has children to raise and things have been extremely hard. His heart has been torn apart, and so have his children's hearts, because they miss the one they love.

This could even be a prayer that is used by someone who has lost literally everything in their life: those that they love, and all of their material possessions except for the clothes on their back. They are in a dark place, full of fear and have lost hope.

This is a prayer asking God for some luck to come into our life. We are asking, through our tears, for Jesus to come down from the heavens and to allow everything to be okay.

It is a very powerful prayer for everyone. It is asking for that river of pain and hurt to be banished. It is asking for a smile to be put back on the faces of our loved ones.

Prayer to Protect Me from Hatred

My guardian angel,
Remind me never to be racist,
Not to feel bitterness, anger or hatred in my
    heart towards others
Or to strike out in violence.
Stop me, my guardian angel, don't let me be
    riled by hatred.
I'm depending on you, my guardian angel.

Let me see that I would be doing wrong
And put love and compassion in my heart.
Thank you, my guardian angel.
Amen.

You are saying a prayer to your guardian angel to help you not to be racist towards another human being. You are asking your guardian angel to protect you from becoming a violent person. You are asking your guardian angel to safeguard your heart with love and compassion.

The world needs a huge amount of love. We all need to allow the love that is inside of us to come forth, to pour out into the world, to stop all the hatred and anger, bitterness and violence.

Prayer to God for My Children

God,
I am grateful for every day.
I humbly ask you to send your angels to
*   surround my children.*
Keep them safe from all harm.
Let them do well in life and be happy.
Thank you, my God.
Amen.

This is a short prayer that Angel Hosus has given me asking for protection for your children, for them to do well in life and to be happy, which is the most important thing that every parent wants for their children. They want their children to have a job and to find love, happiness and joy, to live a fulfilled life. This prayer is asking God for a happy life for your children.

Prayer for God's Love

My guardian angel,
Please talk to God for me.
Tell God, I am grateful for his love.
Every time I lose myself and lose hope
I am so thankful for being able to tap into
*   God.*
Knowing of His love, peace and joy
Gives me hope again.
Thank you, my guardian angel, for helping
*   me.*
Amen.

This is a prayer asking your guardian angel to talk to God for you about how important it is that you are able to tap into God to receive His love, peace and joy. It gives you the confidence you need.

Every time you lose yourself and you lose hope, know that your guardian angel is going to talk to God and remind Him of how important God's love is to you every day of your life.

CHAPTER SIXTEEN

Living Life to The Fullest

Prayer to Thank You for My Soul

Thank you, my God, for sharing part of your-
self with me:
That spark of light and love within my human
body,
My beautiful soul that is part of you,
My God, your love and compassion.
Thank you for my soul of pure love.
Amen.

THIS PRAYER THANKS GOD FOR GIVING YOU PART OF
Himself, that tiny spark of light that is your soul.

Prayer for All the People in
My Life That Help Me Every Day

God,
I eternally thank you
For I would have been lost
Only for all the people that you have put into
    my life.
I ask for you, my God and all your angels, to
    watch over them.
I ask for blessings for them of your love,
    healing, peace and hope.
Amen.

This is a prayer to remind you about all the people that God has put into your life, even if it was only for a short time, who gave you a helping hand. Most of the time we forget about them, whether it's the shopkeeper, your neighbour down the road, or the stranger that helped you. This is just a little prayer thanking God and asking for blessings for them, wherever they may be in the world today.

Prayer for Strength of Mind

My guardian angel,
Please pray to God for me,

Ask Him to strengthen my mind
For it seems to be weak in every way
And makes me vulnerable while making my
*   own decisions.*
Tell God, my guardian angel,
That I thank Him for everything He has given me,
But if He could strengthen my mind even a
*   little bit more, tell God,*
I would be grateful.
Amen.

You are asking your guardian angel to implore God for you to give you strength of mind. It is actually very important. It is something we all need.

A mother and father need to have it in order to guide their children. We all need it in our emotional lives. We need it in our work or when out with friends. We need to have the strength of mind to say yes or say no. There are so many reasons that we need strength of mind.

Many a time you might say to yourself, if only I was stronger, I wouldn't have made that decision. That is strength of mind you are talking about. You didn't listen to your inner self, your soul or your guardian angel prayer. We all need to say this prayer once in a while, so that we have the strength to listen.

Prayer to Sleep

My dearest guardian angel,
It is time for you to put me into a slumber to
sleep.
With your arms and wings tightly around me,
close my eyes
With the light of your fingertips.
As I sleep, watch over and protect me.
When I wake in the morning,
Let me feel good and refreshed,
My loving guardian angel.
Amen.

This is a prayer to say to your guardian angel shortly before you go to bed. Maybe you are already lying in your bed and are under the blankets. You have said your prayers, but you are twisting and turning and not sleeping, or maybe you are ready to fall asleep and are asking for help.

Don't forget to ask for help if you are struggling to fall asleep at night. Just close your eyes and try to relax. Let your guardian angel help you to fall into a deep sleep. Have faith and belief that your guardian angel can help.

Prayer for Being a Messenger

My guardian angel,
Help me to be a messenger for others.
When you, my guardian angel,
Whisper in my ear
Or the soul of a loved one that you have beside
  me
To do something, I usually don't listen, but
  you said, 'Do not be afraid.'
Thank you, my guardian angel, for helping
  me.
Amen.

This beautiful prayer is a way to ask your guardian angel to help you to be a messenger for others, and not to be afraid to do so. Sometimes, strange feelings may come over us and we feel an urge to do something that we might not usually do. This could be to smile at a stranger, or maybe to engage in conversation with someone.

This is the angels, or the souls of our loved ones, using us as messengers to help others. It can be to help friends or family, but it can also be to help a stranger. A thought crosses your mind from your guardian angel, or the soul of their loved ones that your guardian angel has in and around you, asking you to say something. You might think it is silly of you, but don't think that way. Just say it. Remember, never say anything hurtful, because that is not your guardian angel or the soul of a loved one.

We all need those messages in our lives, because they give us hope. This is a prayer asking your guardian angel to help you to be that messenger, to give hope to someone else, because hopefully, one day when you need a message, someone will say something to you that touches your heart and you understand what it means. It may be only two words and you smile. They may mean nothing to the person who has just said them to you, but you hear the message. That is why it is so important to listen to your guardian angel.

If you are being asked to do something that you normally wouldn't do, whether it is to give that smile when you're sitting in a café, or if someone is sitting close to you and you are being told to say hello, just do it. You could say, 'Hello, what a lovely day!' Engage that person in conversation with you, or if someone starts a conversation with you, talk to them.

Sometimes it is their guardian angel or their loved one that has asked them to do so, but the message is not for you. It could be for you to give them a message of some kind through the loving or kind words that you say. So ask your guardian angel to help you to be a messenger.

Prayer for Someone to Love Me

No one loves me,
My guardian angel.
I know you love me
And I thank you for your love.
I know it's unconditional,
But I need human love too.
I feel no one loves me.
I just need someone to tell me they love me.
I just need human arms around me, that
*   human touch of love.*
Let someone tell me they love me today, even
*   a stranger.*
Thank you,
My guardian angel, for loving me.
Amen.

This prayer is a very beautiful and special prayer. All the prayers are, but I have met so many people across the world and of all ages who say to me that no one loves them. It breaks my heart.

Of course, I tell them their guardian angel loves them, and I tell them I love them, too. I give them a hug and they often cry, men and women and children. They tell me that no one has ever told them that they love them, so don't forget to tell those who are in your life that you love them.

Do your best to love the stranger as well. I know I tell people they should say to everybody, 'I love you.' They should say it from the heart. We should all love each other. We should all tell each other and we should have only love and compassion in our hearts.

Remember, the person you are sitting beside on the train or a bus, or passing you by down the street, may feel that no one loves them. Imagine what that feels like, believing that no one in the world loves you or cares for you in any way at all, as if you are merely a bit of dirt on the ground. No one should feel that alone or that isolated. We should all feel connected to each other, because we are all God's children. We are all equal and the same. We are all in need of love. We all need to know someone loves us.

If you are feeling as if no one loves you, I just want to remind you that I love you, even though I don't know you. Your guardian angel loves you too and is always with you and holding on to you tightly.

Prayer for Living Life to the Fullest

My guardian angel implore
My Heavenly Father to instil in me the courage
Not to be afraid of life, but instead to live it,
To climb that mountain and stand at the top,
   to scream and shout,
To swim, to dance and sing,
To love and be loved,
To be still and silent and to listen,
Knowing my Heavenly Father is right there
   with me
And you, my guardian angel, holding on to
   me tightly
While I learn to live life and enjoy it.
Thank you, my guardian angel, for always
   being with me.
Amen.

This is a simple prayer about not being afraid to live life and, even more, to live life each day as if it is your last. It is about doing all the simple things that we do every day, but also enjoying them. Some of them are named in the prayer, the angels said, but I'm sure there are many more.

Your guardian angel wants me to remind you to live for every moment and do all the things you want to do, whether that is going for a run, maybe having a swim if you live by the sea, arranging to meet a friend, or taking a walk. Life is so precious and we must never take it for granted. Although it is sad to think about, one day we will go home to heaven, so we want to make sure that the memories we leave behind are happy ones. We want our children and loved ones to remember us as happy and outgoing and as someone who pushed themselves to live life to the fullest: a happy, caring person, full of love. This prayer is to help you to live each day as if it were your last.

CHAPTER SEVENTEEN

Feeling Unloved

Prayer for Love for a
Mother I Never Knew

My God,
I thank you for the mother I never knew.
Thank you, God,
For taking care of my mother when she carried
   me in her tummy.
I know she must have loved me because I loved her.
I chose her to be my mum
Even though I knew she might not be able to
   take care of me.

I thank you, God,
That she gave birth to me
And gave me up for adoption
So I could be loved and cherished and cared
 for by another mother.
Thank you, my God, for my new mother
Who I love dearly and who means everything
 to me.
She is my mum.
Thank you, God, for the mother I never knew.
Amen.

THIS IS A PRAYER GIVING THANKS TO GOD FOR YOUR BIRTH mother. Most birth mothers give up their child because they have love for their child. They know that they cannot take care of their baby themselves.

It can be for so many other reasons that a mother gives her child up for adoption. It might be because of poverty or fear, or not having the capability to take care of their child themselves. They are almost always doing what they believe to be the best thing for their baby. I know their hearts do get broken. Some birth mothers never have a choice about giving their child away.

Just remember, if not for your birth mother, you would not be here. You chose her to be your birth mother, even though you knew all her circumstances and you knew there was a possibility of her giving you up for adoption. You also knew the mother you are with now at that time, when your soul was in heaven before you were conceived.

Prayer for a Mother's Love

My dearest guardian angel,
Tell God I miss my mother.
He took her home to heaven on my birth.
She never held me in her arms.
Tell God thank you
Because I know my mother's soul is around
  me
Because I feel her love. My guardian angel,
  tell my mother I miss her.
Thank you, God and my guardian angel, for
  allowing me to feel my mother's love.
Amen.

This is a prayer for those who lost their mother at birth, or shortly afterwards, and never knew their mother. It is a prayer for those who always longed for their mother to hold them in their arms.

I remember meeting a young man who told me how he had always longed for his mother to hold him in her arms. I asked why, and he said, 'My mum died when she gave birth to me. She never held me in her arms and, even to this day, I long for it. I know when I marry and have children of my own, I will give my children lots of cuddles and love. Every time I see a baby or young child in its mother's arms, it's as if I become an infant, just for a second, and I want to be held in my mother's arms. I always feel the presence of my mum.'

I knew his mother was looking after him and I thanked God for that.

Prayer for People Who Feel Unloved by Their Parents

Dear God,
I have felt so unloved by my parents.
They never showed any love towards me.
To this day, my God,
I am still devastated by that.
I have always cried out to you, my God,
Saying how could you allow this to happen.
My parents show no affection for me.
God, I'm going to decide now to love my parents
Even if they do not love me.
I'm going to show them love.

> *I'm going to tell them I love them, give them*
>   *a hug.*
> *Even if they push me away. It doesn't matter*
> *Because I know, one day, my God,*
> *They might say I love you too*
> *And that will be the happiest day of my life*
> *But if it doesn't happen,*
> *My God, it's okay.*
> *I have the choice to love my parents.*
> *Thank you, my God,*
> *Amen.*

There are millions of people around the world who have felt unloved by their parents, but if this is true of you, this is a prayer for you. Remember, you can choose to love your parents whether they love you or not. Maybe they don't know how to love. Maybe they have too much resentment within them. Maybe they are afraid to say it, but remember, you have the choice to say you love your parents and to show it.

You can do that in little ways. It is up to you. You don't have to go around allowing yourself to feel unloved by your parents. You can love them, and there is always the hope that one day they will say I love you, too. If your parents are dead, you can hug them spiritually and still tell them you love them.

Prayer to Find Peace Within Myself

Dear guardian angel, help me
To find a way to be with God in my heart,
Not to find that I am in constant conflict
Because of the life I have lived.
I want to feel God's love instead of this enor-
*   mous guilt.*
Help me to find that peace within myself
And God's love
Because without it I have no hope,
My guardian angel.
Amen.

This is a prayer to help us to live a better life, to become closer to God, to be good and honest people, to be truthful and to live a good life. It is about wanting to step away from your old life that was not good. You may have done bad things and you want to change your life. You have turned to God, but you are feeling guilty about your past and you feel that God is judging you. God never judges you, but sometimes we feel that way. You are really finding it hard to feel God's love, and in this prayer you are asking your guardian angel to help you to get closer to God, so you can feel His love and experience that peace within yourself.

When you do yoga or meditate in prayer, or find a

quiet place where you can be silent and still, you can listen and allow the peace and love of God to enter you. You start to lose that uncertainty and find that peace and strength within yourself. You love yourself and are happy. So give yourself a few minutes every day to be there with yourself and your guardian angel doing yoga or meditating in prayer.

You need a space of silence to listen or dance or sing, or you can even go for a walk by the river. Whatever place you need to go for yourself, because God is not judging you for the way you have lived your life. He knows you want to change and get closer and feel His love.

Prayer to God for a Little Help

Dear God,
Again, I have to ask you,
My God, please forgive me,
Burdening you with this request.
God, if you could just send enough money,
     just to pay the bills.
However hard I work, I just fall behind, and
     I am so stressed.
I thank you, God, for everything you have
     done for me.
Amen.

This is a prayer that many of us have to say in our lives, because we all become financially stressed. We either lose our job or the bills pile up. It may have been an emergency within the family. The money went elsewhere and none of the bills got paid. It is a very stressful time for anybody. So in this prayer you are asking God for a little helping hand.

If the thought comes into your mind, go and ask for help. There may be something you are entitled to that will help to pay some of the bills and take part of the stress away, so you can get back on your feet again.

Prayer to God for Forgiveness

My God, please forgive me.
I am always trying to mislead you.
I lie to you all the time,
And yet, I know you love me even though I
*   have been so dishonest.*
God, please continue to help me.
Amen.

This is a short prayer coming from the heart asking for forgiveness from God. You know that God loves you anyway and He knows you are doing your best.

You are asking God to continue helping you and you know He will.

Prayer for My Children

My Lord and my God,
Please forgive me for all my failures.
I feel unworthy to ask you for any favours
But I ask you, my God, for my children,
For a home, food and a good school,
For their emotional well-being, to keep them
*   healthy and safe.*
Please continue to help me, my God.
Amen.

This is a prayer that comes from a parent's heart, and I'd say this prayer comes from every parent across the world calling out to God, probably hundreds of times a year, looking for help. In this prayer, you are telling God that you are not worthy to ask for another favour, but you are asking anyway for your children, for a home, for food, for a good school, for emotional well-being and for them to be healthy and safe. Again, you are asking God to continue helping you. God does not want you to feel unworthy in any way.

You are doing the best you possibly can to be the

best parent you can be and that's what makes you worthy. I know God is smiling down on you, even though you think you are not worthy to ask God of anything. You are God's child. Do you think God would ignore you? He wouldn't. God hears you and He tends to your needs. Sometimes you feel you are not pleased with what God thinks is the best for you. But God will always give what is good for us, even when we cannot see it at the time.

Prayer to Safeguard My Heart

My guardian angel,
Safeguard my heart.
Protect me so that I always keep love and
    compassion
And hope in my heart,
So that I shine with love.
Thank you, my guardian angel.
Amen.

This short prayer is asking your guardian angel to safeguard your heart, to protect it so that you will be loving and compassionate, you will be slow to judge others and will always see the light of hope, and so that you, yourself, shine with the light of love.

Prayer to Help Me Recognise the Important Things

My guardian angel,
Help me to realise and to recognise
That sometimes the little things in my life
Are the most important.
Don't let me miss them
So I won't miss out on the most precious things
* in my life.*
Thank you, my guardian angel, for helping
* me.*
Amen.

This is a prayer asking your guardian angel to help you recognise all the precious little things that happen in your life so that you don't miss out on them, and for you to enjoy them. It is those precious little things that make up your life. When you appreciate them, you smile and laugh more. You give more love, because you love yourself.

Don't wait until something sad happens in your life to understand what the most precious things are: those you love and those who come into your life that you will love as well. It is not the material things. It is the sunshine, the rain, the cold, the wind, the smile.

It's the laughter. It's jumping for joy. It is being loved.

Prayer for a Broken Heart

My dearest guardian angel,
Tell God my heart has been broken.
It has been torn apart.
I feel lost now and so hurt.
I need the light of love to shine in my heart
  again
And the courage and strength now to move
  forward
With your help to find love again.
Thank you for helping me, my guardian angel.
Amen.

This is a prayer for when someone's heart has been broken. When two people have fallen out or separated. When one person says goodbye to the other, whether you're a man or a woman, it is a huge shock to find out that your partner doesn't love you any more.

In this prayer, you are asking your guardian angel to tell God that your heart has been broken and how hurtful it is. You are letting God know that you need the light of love to shine in your heart again and to have the strength and the courage to move forward in your life. You need help to let go of the person you had loved and to wish them the best, because you had loved them.

Love is love and it is very special, whether it lasts for only a short while or for a long time. It is something that we all cherish and search for. Love will come again into your life. Be kind and loving to yourself and your guardian angel will help you to find new love and help you to heal.

CHAPTER EIGHTEEN

The Power of Prayer

Prayer for the Angel of
Hope I Need in My Life

Dear God,
Please keep the Angel of Hope in my life.
Allow me to always see that beacon of light.
Never allow the light of hope to go out.
My God, have the Angel of Hope beckoning
*   to me always*
To keep me following your light of hope,
Giving me the strength and courage I need in
*   my life, but mostly the love.*

Thank you, my God,
Amen.

WE ALL NEED THE ANGEL OF HOPE IN OUR LIVES. THIS IS another reason why I love this prayer. Because of the Angel of Hope, we know that hope makes the impossible possible. The Angel of Hope is a massive angel. There is an enormous flame of light that never goes out, and within this light I see this tremendous angel. I am shown a faint human appearance, which is masculine and of beautiful, emerald-green colours. The Angel of Hope holds this colossal torch flame, something like the Olympic Flame.

The brightness of the Angel of Hope looks different to any other angel. I think this is because he is an angel within a light, within the flame of hope, showing us that the impossible is possible. When there is hope in a person's heart, there is nothing we cannot conquer and overcome with love. It has made us strive towards all the good things of this world.

Many times humanity has tried to destroy hope in order to have control over the people of the world, but God has the Angel of Hope in the world, this particular, wonderful angel. There is only one Angel of Hope, but the Angel of Hope is for each and every one of us.

Prayer for the Power of Prayer

Thank you, God,
For demonstrating the power of prayer in my
life.
You have done this so many times for me.
I thank you, my God and all your angels, a
million times over.
Amen.

This is a simple prayer giving thanks for all those times when prayer was so powerful in your life. You know that you would not have made it through those moments, but for the power of prayer within your life, and the faith and belief you have. You are thanking God a million times over.

The power of prayer can be demonstrated in many ways. The most common examples may be in a healing way, passing an exam, or mending a relationship.

Prayer for the Holy Spirit

Eternal God,
I thank you for every day,
For sending the Holy Spirit to infuse the host
– the bread of life;
Infusing it with God's grace

All over the world.
I love you, my God.
Amen.

This is a prayer about the Last Supper of God, where Jesus shared the bread of life with his family. We are all his family. It is an incredible miracle that happens even to this day at every Mass. When the priest lifts the host, an enormous angel seems to come through his body and lift the host with the priest at the same time, and then this angel takes it to heaven in a flash. It is incredible to see. At the same moment, they meet halfway as the angel carries the host up to heaven, and the light of the Holy Spirit comes down and into the host, infusing it with God's grace of love.

Prayer for Joy in My Life

Please God,
Take this cloud of darkness away.
Shine your light upon me.
Send your angels to help me.
Give me the courage and strength
To start to feel the joy in my life again.
Amen.

This is a prayer to help you to start feeling the joy in your life again. You are asking God to send all His angels to help you.

Prayer to Be My True Self

My guardian angel,
Help me to be truly myself
As I was on the day of my birth,
Uncontaminated by the world,
Full of that potential. How God wants me to
*   be.*
Give me the courage and strength
And I know I can truly be me
With your help, my guardian angel.
Amen.

This is a prayer asking your guardian angel to help you to be yourself, just as you were on the day of your birth, full of pure love and uncontaminated by the world. You were full of the possibilities of goodness. Allow yourself to love and live life with all its ups and downs, but cherish it by being truly yourself.

Prayer of God's Love to Us

I am humble before you, my God, for knowing
I am pure love.
There is no one else in the world like me.
It's okay to love myself.
I am deserving of love.
I choose to love myself more.
There is an abundance of love in my life.
I love myself.
Thank you, my God, for my soul.
Amen.

All of the words that are in this prayer are in my book *Love from Heaven*. This prayer is to remind you of what you already know – that you are pure love because of your soul. You have the capability to put lots of love out into the world, simply by loving yourself more. It doesn't make you greedy or selfish.

As I have said in my book *Love from Heaven*, you cannot love anyone more than you love yourself, so the more you love you, the more love we can put out into the world. Prayer is one way that helps you to love yourself more.

Prayer of Love

Dear God,
Please help me to release
That most precious gift
You have given me of love,
That gift of love
That is connected to my soul.
Amen.

This is a prayer asking God to help you to realise the most precious gift He has given you of love, and how pure you are because of your soul, that spark of light of God. It is part of Him. It can never be contaminated or destroyed in any way. Love cannot be diminished. It is in abundance. It is your soul, that connection to God. The reason why prayer is so powerful is because love is the most overwhelming force in the world. It comes from our soul. It comes from heaven.

It is love that brings happiness and joy into our lives and always steers us in the right direction. It is love that makes living worthwhile. Love brings peace, harmony, and goodwill to us all. Prayer is a loving activity. You are pouring the love from your soul out into the world when you pray, including when you pray with any of the prayers in this book.

Prayer to Love Myself

My guardian angel,
Tell God I need your help.
I need your help
To make a conscious decision to love my own
*   life,*
For me to stop hating my life.
Help me to feel the love of life again.
Remind me, my guardian angel, of the things
*   I love doing.*
Thank you for helping me,
My guardian angel.
Amen.

In this prayer, you are asking your guardian angel to help you make the conscious decision to start to love life again. If you are saying this prayer, you have already started. You want to get out of the habit of not living life, that trap you have fallen into. You want to see the joys that are in your life.

Through this prayer, you are acknowledging to your guardian angel you can do this. You have already made the decision, and you know your guardian angel is going to help you. You are going to be so conscious of every time you say to yourself, or out loud, 'I hate my life.' You will tell yourself, 'No, I can't be saying that any more.' Then you will go and do something you enjoy, to help you to start living life again.

Your guardian angel believes in you, so believe in yourself. You can do it. You can live life again. Start to smile and say to yourself with love and joy, 'I made it.'

Prayer to Say I Love You

Dear God,
Help me, God, to learn to say the words,
I love you,
And for these words to flow from my heart,
And my soul.
Amen.

You can say this prayer to ask God to help you say the words 'I love you' from your heart and your soul, from every particle of you. You are asking God to help you say these three precious words purely to all of those you love, and to all those who will come into your life in the future.

Prayer for the Children of the World

Dear God and my guardian angel,
Help me to help the children of the world
In whatever way I possibly can.

I don't have much but I'm willing to share.
Allow opportunities to come
My way and for me to recognise them with love
So I can contribute to helping the children of
   the world.
Thank you, my God and my guardian angel,
Amen.

This is a prayer asking God and your guardian angel to open your heart, to allow you to help children, no matter what part of the world they live in or what background they are from, what their religion is or whether they are poor or uneducated. They still need your help, no matter how little or how much you have. If we can lend a helping hand to children or to anyone in need, it can mean a lot.

Prayer to Give with a Pure Heart

Lord Jesus,
Instil within me always
To give with a pure heart and expect nothing
   in return.
Amen.

This is a prayer that I am constantly repeating. I say it over and again. To me, it is a beautiful prayer. It is a reminder always to give with a pure heart and expect nothing in return. Every time you go to help someone in any way at all, say this prayer to yourself, so you won't be putting a price on the help that you were giving to someone else. You can't pay for your love, and love helps us to do good deeds, to give someone a helping hand. It doesn't matter if it seems small.

Prayer for my Guardian Angel's Help Today

Help me, my guardian angel,
To do what you ask me to do today.
That is all I ask of you today,
My guardian angel,
Amen.

I love this prayer and I have to smile, because my guardian angel is right here with me, just like yours is with you. My guardian angel told me, 'Say what I say to you, Lorna. Repeat my words.' The angels are doing this all the time for these prayers. They are bringing them from God, but I love this one. It is for all of you from your guardian angels. Your guardian angel will never ask you to do anything that is wrong or that will hurt another human being or nature. Thank you, my guardian angel. This prayer is to help you to listen to your guardian angel when you wake up.

Prayer to Ask for Help to Pray

Archangel Michael,
Please help me to pray
More often,
For I do not pray enough.
I am lazy a lot of the time
And I don't want to bother to pray.
Help me, Archangel Michael, to pray more.
Amen.

This is a short prayer asking Archangel Michael to help you to pray. You are admitting to him that you are lazy a lot of the time and I guess most of us are. To ask Archangel Michael to help us is a good thing, because he is there for us all. The Archangel Michael knows how powerful prayer is.

We must remember that Archangel Michael is on the Throne of God as well. We all have a very special relationship with Archangel Michael. Thank you, Archangel Michael, for this prayer.

CHAPTER NINETEEN

To Open Our Hearts and Defend Against Evil

Prayer to Keep Evil at Bay

*Almighty God, I implore you, our Heavenly
Father,*

*Put the devil in chains. Prevent him from
getting loose in our hearts and in our
minds.*

*Let your love, my God, destroy his wickedness
and barbarism and terror.*

*Every time the devil gets loose in my heart
and my mind,*

Tear him out, my God, with your love.
Thank you, my Eternal Father, my God.
Amen.

THIS PRAYER IS TO HELP YOU, REMINDING YOU TO NOT LET evil into your heart and mind. Every time it creeps in and gets loose, you are asking God to help you to put the wickedness and anger out of your heart and your mind, and to fill them instead with only love. You don't want to become evil yourself or to do something that hurts another human being. We must all remember that love conquers hate.

Prayer to Open Hearts and Minds

My Lord Jesus Christ, my Heavenly Father,
I beseech you to open people's hearts and
    minds
To hear your words of love, conquering and
    destroying hate.
Your love that you bestowed upon us all,
That eternal light of love,
Bringing peace and harmony to all mankind.
Thank you, my God.
Amen.

This is another prayer about evil, whom I call Satan or the devil. That evil has many names throughout many religions and through time itself. When the devil gets loose in our minds and hearts, it fills us with anger and hate and we want revenge.

In today's world, we really need to pray for help for those who have anger and hate in their hearts, those who have allowed the devil to get loose in their minds and in their hearts. We have to help them through prayer and through our own actions of love and compassion to destroy that hate and fill them with love.

Prayer is the only thing that has the power to do that. Nowadays, there is a huge amount of terrorism. We hear of it every day, horrific acts of terrorism upon men, women and children. We cannot allow these horrific acts of violence to destroy the love that is in our own hearts. We cannot allow evil to win, so we must not allow Satan to enter our hearts and minds, no matter how we suffer.

In this prayer, we are asking for the strength and for the grace to keep Satan at bay, to keep him in his chains, for him to be cast down to that place we call hell.

When I say these words, it hurts me. I feel pain in my heart and in my soul, because I feel love and I know God loves Satan and never wanted to do what he had to do. I am feeling the pain and hurt that Our Lord and God feels. It hurts, because I know it doesn't have to be that way.

So I pray all the time for those that are influenced by the other side, those that are doing evil. I pray and ask God for all of those who do these horrible acts of terrorism, of war and of evil, that God will forgive them.

It is hard feeling this pain, and I don't really know how to put it into words, but it is the pain of love. It is love even for those who listen to Satan and allow the devil to get loose in their minds and hearts, because others tell them that the acts of terrorism and war are about love, but they are not.

If you hurt another human being or destroy our world, that is not love, that is not God, that is the other side, that name I don't like to mention, Satan. I am talking about him, because I feel so much pain and hurt in my heart of love for those who do these horrific acts of violence, and at the same time I feel tremendous pain for those who have lost their loved ones and lost everything in their life. It tears my heart apart.

We have to work hard in prayer to keep Satan in chains, to keep him from getting loose in our minds, or influencing others who are using God as a weapon for power and glory for themselves. They want to keep the human race in chains, as slaves to evil, to Satan, to keep us in the darkness.

But God's love shines brightly. It is that radiant light, giving us all hope, knowing we can make this world like a little glimpse of heaven with love, harmony and peace for all mankind. I know evil won't win, because there is an abundance of love in the world, and evil cannot destroy that love, which God keeps growing strong in our hearts through every generation. So pass that love of God on to your children, regardless of your religious beliefs, or whether you believe in God or not.

Love is a powerful force. It opens our minds and hearts to peace and love together as one. Keep that radiant light of hope burning. Prayer, love and hope are the biggest enemy for those who influence others to believe that doing evil is right, for the light of hope cannot be put out, because God put it there.

Prayer for Peace, Love and Harmony

My God,
Bestow upon us,
Love, harmony, and peace for all mankind.
Amen.

This is a simple prayer coming from your heart. It is just a few words, a few thoughts within your mind, asking for love, harmony and peace for all mankind, for everyone. You are putting that love, harmony and peace out into the world through prayer. Many people say to me, 'How can prayer change the world?' This is one way, by putting prayer out into the world.

Say these prayers of love, harmony and peace for everyone with no barriers up. Don't say that someone doesn't deserve it because of the way they live life. When you say a prayer, you can never do that. You must say it with a pure heart, and when you do that, you are allowing your soul to come forward in prayer.

No one needs to know you are in prayer. You can pray anywhere, even in the noisiest room, or at a football match or at the pictures. Even when you are holding someone you love in your arms, you can pray and ask for protection for them. Prayer can be said anywhere: in the middle of the street or in a hospital bed or a prison cell. Prayer has no barriers.

Prayer of Praise

Holy God, I love you.
I praise and honour your holy name.
Glory to you, my God, from the heavens.

I bow down before you, my God, with an
    open heart of love.
I praise you and love you for eternity.
Thank you for your love, my God.
Amen.

This is a prayer expressing your own personal love to
God. Your love to God can be shown in so many
different ways: by living life to the fullest, by enjoying
and appreciating all of the blessings and gifts He has
given you, by allowing yourself to be happy and keeping
that light of God's love shining from you as a beacon
for others of hope, by being kind and gentle, and by
showing God's love in the world through your actions.

Prayer for Help

Come, Lord Jesus,
I need your help now. I am lost.
Please help me to do the work
I have to do today.
Amen.

Prayer to the Archangel Michael

Archangel Michael,
Protect me and guide me with your sword and
    shield,

Light up the path of my life that is ahead of
    me
Through all my triumphs and disappoint-
    ments.
I know you are there, Archangel Michael,
When I need you, thank you.
Amen.

This is a prayer to the Archangel Michael expressing that you know he is there when you need him. This prayer is all about acknowledging within yourself the path of your life that is ahead of you, with all the triumphs and disappointments. It gives you comfort that God has the Archangel Michael in the world, not only for you, but for everyone. You are thanking the Archangel Michael for carrying that sword and shield as he does all the time.

Prayer to the Archangel Raphael

Archangel Raphael, I implore you
To ask God to send His Healing Angels
To all the places in the world that are full of
    conflict, and to bring peace.
We need your help, Archangel Raphael. Please
    ask God to send you.
We need you to come.

Thank you,
Archangel Raphael.
Amen.

This is a prayer asking for the help of Archangel Raphael for our world. You are asking him to ask God to send all the Healing Angels. I guess the most important part of this prayer is that you are asking for all the conflict to be destroyed in our world and for peace to come. In a gentle way, we are pleading with Archangel Raphael to ask God if he could come to help, because we feel in our hearts that we need Archangel Raphael.

Prayer for Forgiveness and Peace of Mind

God,
Please forgive me for all my imperfections,
For all the wrongs I have done.
Give me the grace to forgive those that have
hurt me.
Amen.

This is a short prayer telling God that you acknowledge all your imperfections within yourself. In this prayer, you are really asking God to help you to forgive yourself. God is not judging. The forgiveness that flows out of us for other people gives us the space to forgive ourselves and to move on in life.

You are asking as well for God's love, because you are asking Him to give you the grace to forgive those who have hurt you, as you have done the same to others, and you no longer want to be like that. You don't want to hurt others. You want to rise above it. You want God to fill you with the grace of love and the strength you need to rise above hurting others, so you can be the good, kind and loving person you really are.

Prayer to Allow My Soul to Get Closer to God

My glorious God,
I ask you to inspire me, to guide me, to lead
  me
Down the path of finding the spirituality
  within me –
My soul. I want to get closer to you,
My God, in every way.
Allow my spirituality to grow so I can get
  closer to you, my God,
To become a kinder and more loving person.
I love you, my God.
Amen.

This is a prayer asking for your spirituality to grow. It is a prayer that I get many requests for. I think God has given me more than one of these prayers, but we should never be afraid to ask God to allow our spirituality to grow so that we can grow closer to God Himself, because the closer you are to God, the more loving and caring you will be. Life gets simpler as you become full of peace.

CHAPTER TWENTY

Living A Fulfilled Life

Prayer to Call for Help

God, please help me now.
Mary, my Mother, Queen of the Heavens,
My guardian angel and all the angels, and all
  the heavenly saints,
I need your help. Please help.
Thank you for your help.
Amen.

MANY A TIME WE CALL OUT IN PRAYER OURSELVES. WE
call out from the depths of our heart, asking God,
all the angels, the saints, and Mary, Our Mother to

help us. We do this often throughout our lives, even people who don't call themselves religious. We are always calling on God's help.

Prayer for Jesus, Mary, Help Us

Jesus, Mary, please help.
Don't forsake us.
Jesus, Mary,
What is happening? Help us.
Amen.

The angels are telling me that the words used in this prayer are said in many languages and from people of different religions throughout the world. When something horrific has happened in our lives, we use these words.

I recognise them from when I was a young child and I saw my grandmother call out in this way when she found her son lying on the floor unconscious. They were surrounded by all of the angels. I stood over in the corner, praying and asking God to please allow my uncle to be okay. My uncle was whisked away by the doctor in all the commotion.

The next day when I was in the house, my grandmother was making a cup of tea and thanking everyone for their help and then she said another prayer.

Prayer to Thank You

Thank God
He is okay.
Amen.

The words of a prayer can be so short. It can be just one word, but it is where that word of prayer comes from that matters. This prayer came from my grandmother's heart and her soul. It was said with the love that she has for her son. This prayer was said in pure love.

This prayer can be said for anyone. It could be for a family, a friend, a love, a son, a daughter, a husband or a wife, or you could say it for strangers.

Prayer from a Mother to Stop Bullying

God, I am knocking on your door.
Please don't forsake me.
I need you to hear my prayer, my God,
Not for my sake but for my child's.
They are being bullied.
They are terrified and never stop crying.
My child says they wish they were dead.
Please God, help me to find those who can
*   help my child*
Before it's too late.

Thank you, my God,
My guardian angel and all the angels for your help.
Amen.

God has given many prayers like this one for us to say. It is not only for a parent or a grandparent to say. Friends, strangers, even children can use it. We can all say this prayer, because there are so many children in the world today who are being bullied, and many of them have found life so horrific and terrifying they have taken their own life when they couldn't bear it any more. This prayer is asking for help and especially it asks for those who can come to the aid of these children to help them.

I receive letters from parents, from grandparents, and even sometimes from the children themselves telling me of the horrific abuse they are receiving from other children in school. Even after they go to big school when they are teenagers, this bullying continues, but they tell me that knowing they have a guardian angel helps.

Young children from the age of six to teenage years, and even those at college, describe how having a guardian angel has helped them tremendously, especially when they have been bullied. They tell me how they ask their guardian angel to ask the guardian angel of the child or the young person who is bullying them to help them. They say it works every time. Many a time, the child will tell me in a letter that those who were bullying them have now become their friend.

Here is a little extract from one letter from a young teenager:

> One day, my mum suggested to me to read your book *Angels in My Hair*. I read it, and just thinking that everyone has a guardian angel made me see the world differently. In my school, the other kids bully me and make me feel like I want to give up on life. It has been horrible. I just want to die, but knowing they too have a guardian angel, just like me, that can help them to grow up as a person helps. Your book has made me have compassion and understanding that they are human beings, instead of me wanting to make them suffer. I look on everything differently now and my guardian angel has been a great help. For now, I have wonderful friends and I am happy. I no longer want to die.

This prayer is important for us all to say, whether we have children or not. There could be a child or a young teenager or young person at college being bullied, who is lonely, who has no friends and is having a horrible time. They may find that they cannot cope and just want to die.

Their guardian angel is doing everything and so is God and all the angels to shine that light of hope in front of them, but you and I must be that light of hope as well. No one wants young people or children to take their own life because of bullying. It is a terrifying, violent and horrific thing to live with every day. The child or young person can take only so much.

If you can help, please do. Be that light of hope. That young girl's mum gave my book *Angels in My Hair* to her young daughter and told her to read it. It made her look on the world differently, knowing she had a guardian angel. She has hope that those who are bullying her will grow up kind and loving, and will realise they have a guardian angel, too.

Prayer for Belief

God, help me to believe in you.
I want to have faith. I want to believe
In you, my God.
I pray and pray.
I know it's on me to believe in you, my God.
Amen.

This is a prayer if you are finding it so hard to believe in God, to believe you have a soul and a guardian angel. You are constantly saying to yourself, 'If there was a God, none of this would be happening to me.' Yet you are praying in desperation, wanting to believe that there is a God, that life is worth it. You are asking God to help you to believe, because in your heart you know there is a God, but the world and life itself is trying to destroy your faith with all of its violence and hatred.

You don't want to be part of that violence or hatred. You want to belong to God. You want to be free to love, to feel kindness and joy, to be happy and to help others have love and happiness. You know it is okay to believe in God, your soul and your guardian angel.

Prayer for Self-love and Inner Strength

My guardian angel,
Help me to go in search of my soul
For my self-love
And the inner strength that dwells within my soul.
Thank you for helping me,
My guardian angel.
Tell God I love Him.
Amen.

This prayer helps you to acknowledge your soul and the self-love and strength that dwells within you. You are asking your guardian angel to help you to find that love and strength, to allow it to come forward.

Do not be afraid of the self-love that you have. It is in abundance because your soul, that spark of light of God, is never-ending love that is pure and real. You can love yourself and love others freely and be loved, because you will discover that you are pure love.

Prayer to Open the Door to Life Again

My guardian angel,
Archangel Michael too, please help me.
I'm so tired and weary.
I have lost interest in life itself,
And just want to be left alone.
Please help me to open the door to life again.
Thank you,
Amen.

This is a prayer that I suppose we all need to say at those times of our lives when we feel life has become so overwhelming and we are tired. We just want to close the door. I would say to you, have a rest and ask your guardian angel and the Archangel Michael and all the angels of God to give you a helping hand to open the door again to life. Then take that little rest. You need it.

Prayer for Courage and Strength

God,
I just want to tell you I believe in you.
I know you have always been there for me,
Even at times when I thought I was lost,
God, you always gave me the courage and
  strength I needed.
Thank you, my God.
Amen.

This is another short prayer giving thanks to God, because you believed in Him even when you felt lost and lonely, or at a time in your life when you felt desperate or brokenhearted. You still believed, knowing that God would give you the courage and strength to get through that situation in your life.

You were asking God for a sign and you received it. You didn't put up any barriers and then you gave thanks to God. You are saying, 'I don't have to do anything alone any more and that is because my guardian angel is right there with me.'

One of the most common signs that God gives is

for a person to feel the presence of God or to hear God's voice talk to them.

As well as that, others will come into your life and you will find courage to ask them for help when you need it, so you don't have to do everything alone.

Prayer for Another Chance for the World

God,
I am always asking you for just one more chance
And you are always giving them to me,
But now, my God, I don't ask for myself.
I ask you, my God,
Can you give our world another chance.
Amen.

In this prayer, you are asking God to give our world another chance to make things right. Just like God has done for you on umpteen occasions throughout your life. We can all look back on our lives as individuals and see that divine pattern, where God and the angels have given us a hand and helped us to find that second chance. Sometimes we have to go back in time in our mind and look through our life, to begin to recognise all those occasions that God gave us another chance.

In this prayer, you are not asking that for yourself, but you are asking for mankind, all of mankind. This is a beautiful prayer that God has given me to share with you.

Prayer to the Angel of Mother's Love

Dear God,
Would you please have the Angel of Mother's
   Love around me
For I need to feel a mother's love today,
As my own mother is in heaven with you.
Have the Angel of Mother's Love around me.
Thank you, my God.
Amen.

You are asking God to have the Angel of Mother's Love around you. You may not know whether your mother loved you or not. You may know your mother loved you very much. Sometimes a mother does not know how to show their child love, because it was never shown to them. So the Angel of Mother's Love is letting you know that your mother loved you and this is very important to us all.

The Angel of Mother's Love is very beautiful. The only way I can describe her is that she is like a mother hen with her arms and wings wrapped around you, pouring into you the love of a mother, helping you to feel a mother's love.

Prayer to Love Those I Don't Like

My dearest guardian angel,
Tell God I'm grateful for everything.
Please help me to give a little love to others
   today,
Especially to those who I am angry with
Or those I dislike. Help me,
My guardian angel, to give them a little love.
Thank you, my guardian angel, for helping
   me.
Amen.

You are asking your guardian angel to help you with a particular task each day of your life – to give a little love to others, especially to those you may be angry with, disappointed with or dislike. If you show a little love and kindness towards them, it will help heal your wounds. If you show others love and kindness, you create a sacred space within yourself where love and kindness can flow into you. It will help you to stop locking your love away. That means you will stop hurting yourself as well.

Show them a little kindness and a little love. Forgive, even a little bit at a time, so that you get used to forgiving. Giving a little love is precious and has no price. So give a little love today.

Prayer for My Guardian Angel Who is With Me Every Day

My guardian angel,
I know you take me by the hand every day
And because of that
I know I'm not alone.
Thank you, my guardian angel,
For being with me every day of my life through
*   eternity.*
Amen.

This is a prayer thanking your guardian angel for taking your hand every day and leading you through life, for simply being there with you. This prayer gives you the comfort of knowing your guardian angel is holding your hand and that you are not alone. No matter where you are or what is happening in your life, know that your guardian angel has your hand in their hand. Let it give you comfort knowing you are loved.

Prayer to Help Me Be a Good Samaritan

God,
Help me to be a good Samaritan
As often as I possibly can be.
Amen.

This little prayer is asking God to help you to be a good Samaritan, because you know, in your heart, that one day you could be depending on someone to be a good Samaritan to you. You hope that they would not turn away and say to themselves that they don't care.

You know, in your heart, that you need to be a good Samaritan in every situation, no matter how small it may be, because you might need someone's help tomorrow.

CHAPTER TWENTY-ONE

You Can Pray Anywhere

I HAVE COME TO THE END OF THIS PRAYER BOOK AND I hope it touches all your hearts and helps to teach you how to pray. You can be in prayer anywhere. You don't have to go to a special place. A moment of silence allows your soul to come forward and helps you to drift into a meditative state of prayer, bringing you closer to God. You never pray alone, because all the angels pray with you.

Your prayers are words coming from you as a human being, but as you go into a deep state of prayer, you hear the words coming from your soul. You experience your soul in the depths of prayer. This can happen even if you sing in prayer, or if you dance in prayer, or meditate. There are loads of ways people pray, but no matter how you pray, you are allowing yourself to be fully joined to your soul. You are going into a state of prayer that you have never been in before.

You may only experience it for a few moments in human terms, but for your soul that would have been like eternity. It loves when you decide to pray. Your soul is pure love and, because of that, prayer is powerful in ways we cannot imagine.

Prayer is extremely important for our physical body and our minds, that emotional side of us, which each and every one of us struggles with at different times within our lives. Use the power of prayer to help you get through those times. Allow your soul to become more connected to your physical body and your mind. Allow the power of prayer to help you to heal your physical body and your mind. Allow that intertwining of the body and soul.

From the beginning of time, from that moment God fell in love with us and gave us that tiny speck of Himself, our soul, we have been in search of the spiritual side of ourselves. We didn't understand it, but we were conscious and aware that we had a spiritual side. We may have called it something else.

I don't know when we started to recognise that it was our soul, but we were in search of it and we still are today.

We have many rituals through all religions. We sacrificed animals and sometimes even other human beings in the hope of finding our spiritual self, our souls. To find God, we fasted, went without food for days, or had torture inflicted upon ourselves. We danced, we sang, we went into trances and took drugs. We went down into the bowels of the earth in search of the afterlife. We still do some of those things but, as the centuries passed, we learnt gradually that we did not have to offer up sacrifices. We did not have to inflict torture on ourselves or on others.

We learnt that we could find God, our soul, our spiritual selves through the power of prayer. We did not have to do what they did in ancient times, but we do need to pray today. You and I need prayers from others, and you and I need to pray every day. It takes only a moment. We must all pray so that we can make this world like a little glimpse of heaven, so the intertwining of the human body and the soul can happen. We would no longer become sick, our souls would shine brightly, and we would all see the souls of everyone around us. We would know that God is real.

God *is* real. Don't wait until it is your time to go

home to heaven to discover that. Discover it now through the power of prayer, and realise that God is real. He has given you a guardian angel who is the gatekeeper of your soul. Allow your soul to look out through your physical eyes and see the world differently, in a positive, beautiful way, for your life is blessed through the power of prayer and knowing that God is real.

If the human race all prayed together for one minute right across the world, with all religions and none, and those whom we consider good or bad, it would change everything for ever.

A prayer can be anything you want it to be. You can recite a prayer that you know or speak to God in your own words. The prayers in this book were given by God to His angels to give to me. God has given His permission to share them with you and your loved ones. God puts up no barriers and neither do the angels; anyone can pray.

I have asked the angels to rush forward to heaven to implore God for a miracle in all of your lives.

All my blessings and love to you all.

Lorna

The List of Prayers

Acknowledgements

A heartfelt thanks to my daughter, Aideen Byrne, for editing the prayer book, for her support and dedication, for being there by my side while writing this book and for all her enormous hard work.

Mark Booth, my Publisher, thank you for all your support and encouragement over the years. Thank you for the days you spent with me Aideen, doing the final edit of the prayer book. Without you both, I would never have managed as I am severely dyslexic – thank you for all your patience.

I want to thank my daughter, Pearl Byrne, for all the help as my agent and for her constant dedication, encouragement and support.

My heartfelt thanks to my loving family for all the support and encouragement. I wouldn't be able to do what I do, only for you. Thank you from the depths of my heart.

Thank you to the Art Department at Hodder & Stoughton for the cover of the prayer book – it looks so magnificent.

Thank you from the bottom of my heart to the sales team here in Ireland and in England.

Thank you, Suzi Button, for all your encouragement and your hard work as the Manager of the Lorna Byrne Children's Foundation.